"Avoiding the errors of those who propose Christ's assumption of a fallen nature, Bello offers a lucid account of how the Son's human nature is actually sanctified. Furthermore, by seriously considering the Trinitarian nature of the act of assumption, the reader is treated to a careful and nuanced construction of a model rejecting the fallen view. Learned in the christological thinking of Thomas Aquinas and Karl Barth, this study warrants serious consideration."

—Christopher R. J. Holmes,
associate professor of systematic theology,
head of the theology programme,
University of Otago (New Zealand)

"This question, whether the human nature assumed by the Son is fallen or unfallen, is one of the most vexed and complicated questions in theology. Bello's argument here is a fine piece of theological research, approaching modern discussions by bringing into play patristic (inseparable operations), medieval (the grace of union), and Protestant scholastic (federal headship) resources."

—Fred Sanders,
Torrey Honors Institute,
Biola University

SINLESS FLESH

A Critique of Karl Barth's Fallen Christ

STUDIES IN HISTORICAL
H
S ✠ S
T
& SYSTEMATIC THEOLOGY

SINLESS FLESH

A Critique of Karl Barth's Fallen Christ

RAFAEL NOGUEIRA BELLO

STUDIES IN HISTORICAL AND SYSTEMATIC THEOLOGY

LEXHAM PRESS

Sinless Flesh: A Critique of Karl Barth's Fallen Christ
Studies in Historical and Systematic Theology

Copyright 2020 Rafael Nogueira Bello

Lexham Press, 1313 Commercial St., Bellingham, WA 98225
LexhamPress.com

Print ISBN 9781683594055
Digital ISBN 9781683594062
Library of Control Control Number 2020938443

Lexham Editorial: Todd Hains, Eric Bosell, Michael Haykin
Cover Design: Bryan Hintz
Typesetting: Danielle Thevenaz, Abigail Stocker

For my mother and father, Elaine and Edson

Eu amo vocês.

CONTENTS

ACKNOWLEDGMENTS

The current work is a slightly modified version of my PhD dissertation. I have many people to acknowledge for this project. Starting with my mentors, Jonathan Pennington has been a great fountain of encouragement for me from the beginning of my career as a theologian. Stephen Wellum has patiently listened to my ideas. Christopher Holmes has showed me the character of a true scholar, emphasizing that the lonely and patient work with primary sources is always better than quick secondary source references. Having worked in the library for several years of my graduate studies, I am especially thankful for the librarians who made this work possible: Ryan Vasut, Christi Osterday, and C. Berry Driver have all helped me both finding and acquiring new materials. Their patience with me is a virtue to be modeled. The community of Third Avenue Baptist Church has also flooded my family and me with love. I also have an immense debt to the late John Webster. As I was flirting with other approaches to theology it was reading his work that my love for God was rekindled.

I am also grateful to the community of learners at The Southern Baptist Theological Seminary. Countless conversations over coffee at 2:30 p.m. in the doctoral common room were essential for shaping this work. Friends like Trey Moss, Darron Chapman, Shawn Wilhite, Paul Gesting, Andrew Ballitch, Jonathan Kiel, Jacob Denhollander, Garrick Bailey, Richard Blaylock, Lucas Sabatier, Oren Martin, Kyle Claunch, Chris Smith, Tyler Wittman, and many others have helped me shape this book through content or emotional and spiritual encouragement. This book was also possible because of conversations with theologians and friends that I only know online. Michael Allen kindly read the portion of this work that engages with him and provided me some insights in email conversations. Others who directly or indirectly helped me are Nathaniel Gray Sutanto, Greg W. Parker, Christopher Wozniki, Adonis Vidu, Darren Sumner, and many others that space prevents my listing. My friends from Brazil have also made my journey much lighter by always making me laugh and by asking good questions. They are Claudio Cordeiro, Esdras Pinto, Marcos Oliveira, André Carvalho, André "Pet" Guedes, Thiago "Cebola" Martinello, Lucas Carvalho, Charles Grimm, Marcos Grimm, Bruno Inglês, Eduardo "Maninho" Néris, Davi Peres, and Diogo Agum.

I am beyond grateful to my wife, Josie. She has taken the herculean task of parenting our beautiful children, Clara, Natalia, and Thomas while I was working on this book. Not only has she been doing great in parenting, but she showed herself to be an excellent and wonderful companion during this time. Furthermore, my mom and my dad (to whom I dedicate this book) have both given me so much support that another book would need to be written in order to thank them. Finally, I am grateful to the Lord Jesus Christ. As I write this, I am made even more aware of his covenantal presence and his care for me and my family. "Now to him who is able to keep you from stumbling, and to present you blameless before the presence of his glory with great joy, to the only God, our Savior, through Jesus Christ our Lord, be glory, majesty, dominion, and authority, before all time and now and forever. Amen" (Jude 24–25).

Rafael Nogueira Bello
São José dos Campos, Brazil
February 2020

ABBREVIATIONS

—

CD	Barth, Karl. *Church Dogmatics*, 4 vols. Edinburgh: T&T Clark, 1956–1975.
IJST	*International Journal of Systematic Theology*
Mod. Theol.	*Modern Theology*
PRRD	Muller, Richard A. *Post-Reformation Reformed Dogmatics: The Rise and Development of Reformed Orthodoxy, Ca. 1520 to Ca. 1725*, 4 vols. Grand Rapids: Baker Academics, 2003.
RD	Bavinck, Herman. *Reformed Dogmatics*, 4 vols. Ed. John Bolt. Trans. John Vriend. Grand Rapids: Baker Academic, 2006.
SBJT	*The Southern Baptist Journal of Theology*
SCG	*Summa Contra Gentiles.* Turnhout: Brepols Publishers, 2010.
SJT	*Scottish Journal of Theology*
ST	Aquinas, Saint Thomas. *Summa Theologiae: Complete Set*. Ed. The Aquinas Institute. Lander, WY: The Aquinas Institute, 2012.
Works	Owen, John. *The Works of John Owen*. Edinburgh: Banner of Truth, 1965.
WTJ	*Westminster Theological Journal*

1

INTRODUCTION

Purity is passé now. Purity culture has been denounced by former proponents (maybe rightly so) and to call someone a puritan has degrading con-
notations. I have no doubt that much has been done in the name of purity
in order to exploit the weak and to abuse power. Today, solidarity, authen-
ticity, and identification are probably more prized than purity. People do
not want Mr. Perfect's help because Mr. Perfect cannot understand their
struggles and mistakes. Over the past few years, Christological studies
have been forced to decide between identification and purity. The question
motivating this study is, must one choose between the two?

Central to this question is the human nature of Christ. Various con-
troversies regarding the humanity of the Savior have loomed over the
church, reflecting on this matter. As early as the first century, gnostic
tendencies challenged the goodness of created human nature and therefore provoked responses from biblical authors.[1] Early church councils also
dealt with issues regarding Christ's human nature. Apollinarianism and
Monophysitism held to some deficient notions of the humanity of the
Savior.[2] It is in the context of defending the Nicene trinitarian Christology
against Apollinarian tendencies that Gregory of Nazianzus penned the
words, "that which He has not assumed He has not healed" (Τὸ γὰρ
ἀπρόσληπτον, ἀθεράπευτον ὃ δὲ ἥνωται τῷ Θεῷ, τοῦτο καὶ σώζεται; *nam
quod assumptum non est, curationis est expers*).[3] Opponents of Apollinarianism
made this phrase by Gregory an axiom against the insistence that the soul

---

1. See Urban C. von Wahlde and Chris Keith, *Gnosticism, Docetism, and the Judaisms of the
First Century: The Search for the Wider Context of the Johannine Literature and Why It Matters*
(New York: Bloomsbury T&T Clark, 2016).

2. Aloys Grillmeier, *Christ in Christian Tradition: From the Apostolic Age to Chalcedon*
(Louisville, KY: Westminster John Knox Press, 1988), 47.

3. Gregory of Nazianzus, Epistle 101 (Epistle 1 to Cleodonius), in *A Select Library of the
Nicene and Post-Nicene Fathers of the Christian Church*, 28 vols. in two series, ed. Philip Schaff

of Christ is somewhat substituted by the divine person. In the following debate the same phrase is used, but to argue for another substitution.

In the nineteenth and twentieth centuries, a claim arose out of the German and English-speaking worlds. Several theologians asserted that the Son of God assumed a fallen human flesh mainly because he had to assume what was natural in our humanity. To be clear, the theologians who made such claims and the ones who will be covered in this study have not said that Christ sinned, but that his nature was one like humankind after the fall. The doctrine of Christ's assumption of a fallen flesh (henceforth, *non-assumptus*) was made known by British theologian Edward Irving (1792–1834). Irving emphasized the role of the Spirit in the incarnation and was even charged with heresy by his contemporaries.[4]

Since the charge of heresy is often raised in this debate, it should be pointed that this present work does not aim to charge anyone with heresy.[5] There are a few ways one can construe the relationship of the Son and his humanity and still remain orthodox. It is especially telling that many advocates of the *non-assumptus* (especially the ones surveyed here) also assert that the Son did not sin even if united to a sinful flesh. It is the concern of both sides of the debate to be fair to texts such as Hebrews 4:15. Christ must be said to be like us in every way, but also, to *be without sin*.

One cannot cover every position and nuance regarding the possibility of the human nature of Christ and sin. In order, however, to lay the subject at hand in a better purview, I will use the Sykes-Hastings taxonomy of affirmations used by E. Jerome van Kuiken in order to facilitate the analysis of those who affirm the *non-assumptus*:

1. *Prior to the conception, the humanity of Christ existed in Mary in a state of original sin;*

2. *At the time of conception, the humanity of Christ was transformed;*

---

et al. (Buffalo, NY: Christian Literature, 1887–1894), series 2, 7:440; *Patrologia cursus completus, Series Graeca*, 161 vols., ed. J.-P. Migne (Paris: Migne, 1857–1866), 37:181–84.

4. See Colin E. Gunton, "Two Dogmas Revisited: Edward Irving's Christology," SJT 41, no. 3 (1988): 161–63.

5. Any accusation of heresy that goes beyond ecumenical confessions and ecclesial division (in the case for the doctrine of justification, separating Roman Catholics and Protestants) has the *onus probandi* resting on the accuser.

3. *During Jesus's earthly ministry he suffered the amoral effects of the fall, but not the moral corruption: He was hungry, sad, sick;*

4. *Whatever one means by fallenness, it cannot mean that he sinned or has personal guilt.*[6]

This grid should allow one to read proponents of the *non-assumptus* charitably, even when disagreeing with them. What remains then is to dispute issues like the manner and trinitarian character of assumption, sanctification, and the nature of sin and corruption. So, we start here with a basic notion of human nature and then follow the next chapters discussing deeper and more complex issues.

WHAT IS A HUMAN NATURE?
A CHALCEDONIAN-THOMISTIC ACCOUNT

Foundational to the debate of whether Christ had a *fallen human nature* is a deeper discussion of what is a human nature. It is only normal that many points of departure are possible. In fact, it has been argued for a while that we should abandon church-imposed dogmas on what constitutes a human being (person and nature).[7]

This work, however, listens attentively to the church. Not with a presupposed distrust, or chronological snobbery, but with an initial trust that the rehashing of concepts regarding nature, person, grace, etc., has been

---

6. E. Jerome Van Kuiken, *Christ's Humanity in Current and Ancient Controversy: Fallen or Not?* (New York: Bloomsbury T&T Clark, 2017), 165–66.

7. John Hick, *The Myth of God Incarnate* (London: Hymns Ancient & Modern Ltd, 1977):"For many people, the incarnation of God in Jesus Christ is the essence of Christianity. Without the incarnation, Christianity would be something else. Yet this assumption is open to a great many questions, and in one of the most exciting and provocative collections of studies to appear for a long time, a group of theologians asks whether the idea of the incarnate God is not another of those patristic doctrines which need to be criticized and interpreted afresh in the modern world. The prospect may sound sensational and destructive, but this volume has neither characteristic. It has been produced by distinguished scholars, who examine the evidence from the New Testament onwards with care and thoroughness. And as they ask their questions, they are at the same time concerned with the consequences of their findings for a full and living Christian faith today. Their work is something that no thinking Christian can ignore.There are ten essays in all, written by the editor, and by Don Cupitt, Michael Goulder, Leslie Houlden, Dennis Nineham, Maurice Wiles and Frances Young.

guided and directed by the Holy Spirit. In such fashion, we have conceptual tools to help us talk—at least minimally—about human nature, starting with the One who reveals nature to us.[8]

Since Chalcedon solidified the talk about the human nature of Christ, it is only fitting that we start with this council. Sarah Coakley provides three possible readings of the Chalcedonian definition.[9] The first is a *linguistically regulatory* view. According to this view, the council was not particularly setting an ontology of the person-nature distinction, but merely establishing parameters for predication. The second view is associated with John Hick. Here Chalcedon is seen only as *metaphorical* and in no way regulatory. The third option, proposed by Coakley, is the *literal* view. Here, Chalcedon provides something true about person and nature—in Christ. This, in some fashion, provides the possibility of ontological speech about the person of Christ, even if the details are not precisely discussed.[10]

Following the *literalist* view, we can say that the council makes a fundamental assertion that is later picked up regarding the development of natures and person in dogmatic theology. Even if not fully developed in AD 451, concepts such as natures and persons are cohesively developed following the parameters set by Chalcedon and Nicaea. The work of Brian Dailey on Leontius of Byzantium[11] and of Hans Urs von Balthasar on Maximus the Confessor[12] showcase the consistent development of the *an-en-hypostasis* and dyotheletism within the parameters of Chalcedon.

Developments of Chalcedonian dogma were not restricted to 551 (Constantinople II) and 681 (Constantinople III). The Scholastic period

---

8. See Marc Cortez, *Christological Anthropology in Historical Perspective: Ancient and Contemporary Approaches to Theological Anthropology* (Grand Rapids: Zondervan, 2016); Marc Cortez, *ReSourcing Theological Anthropology: A Constructive Account of Humanity in the Light of Christ* (Grand Rapids: Zondervan, 2018); Aaron Riches, "Christology and Duplex Hominis Beatitudo: Re-Sketching the Supernatural Again," *IJST* 14, no. 1 (January 2012): 44–69.

9. Sarah Coakley, "What Does Chalcedon Solve and What Does It Not? Some Reflections on the Status and Meaning of the Chalcedonian Definition," in *The Incarnation: An Interdisciplinary Symposium on the Incarnation of the Son of God*, ed. Stephen T. Davis, Daniel Kendall, and Gerald O'Collins (Oxford: Oxford University Press, 2004), 143–63.

10. Thanks to Darron Chapman for pointing me to this essay.

11. Brian E. Daley SJ, ed., *Leontius of Byzantium: Complete Works* (New York: Oxford University Press, 2017).

12. Hans Urs von Balthasar, *Cosmic Liturgy: The Universe According to Maximus the Confessor* (San Francisco: Ignatius Press, 2003). See also Pauline Allen and Brownen Neil, ed., *The Oxford Handbook of Maximus the Confessor* (New York: Oxford University Press, 2015).

(roughly 1100–1700) saw an increase of questions regarding the God-World relationship that largely reflected on Christology.[13] Thomas Aquinas (*Doctor Angelicus*) reflected on the modes of sanctification that can be attributed to Christ and also discussed human nature in a long philosophical reflection in *prima pars*. These were extended meditations that tried to preserve the concepts handed down from Chalcedon. Aquinas, however, did not contradict or develop his doctrines of sanctification apart from Chalcedon.

It is true that Aristotelian metaphysics played its part in Aquinas's development of nature, essences, and existences, but that should not hinder us from appreciating the approach. Although Scripture gives general guidelines for metaphysical approaches, in several instances, Scripture does not determine what metaphysical approach one should take. As long as no contradiction arises, appropriation of a certain Greek formulation does not invalidate or undermine the philosophical-theological approach.[14] Moreover, Aquinas does not uncritically receive Aristotle's formulation, but Christianizes it in order to make sense of biblical data.[15]

Foundational for this discussion is Thomas Aquinas's concept of essences and existences. St. Thomas explains that created reality has a fundamental difference between *esse* and *essentia*.[16] By doing that, Thomas

---

13. On the God-World relationship and scholastic theology (epitomized in Thomas Aquinas), see Christopher R. J. Holmes, "Revisiting the God/World Difference," *Mod. Theol.* 34, no. 2 (October 27, 2017): 159–76.

14. Paul J. Griffiths, *Decreation: The Last Things of All Creatures* (Waco, TX: Baylor University Press, 2014), 35–59.

15. The Thomistic-Aristotelian approach does not run uncritically in the Christian tradition. Thomas Torrance claims that Thomas does not pay sufficient attention to the biblical testimony and uncritically imposes a Greek metaphysical grid in the Bible, but, as Thomas White said, "St. Thomas's critical evaluations and use of the Aristotelian corpus (and other ancient and medieval philosophical authors) are influenced by his theological perspective in important ways that seek to adapt the insights of philosophical science to the truths of revelation." Thomas Joseph White, *Wisdom in the Face of Modernity: A Study in Thomistic Natural Theology* (Ave Maria, FL: Sapientia Press, 2009), 76.

16. St. Thomas says, "Separated intellectual substances are not composed of matter and form; rather, in them the form itself is a subsisting substance; so that form here is that which is and being itself [*esse*] is act and that by which the substance is. And on this account there is in such substances but one composition of act and potency, namely the composition of substance and being [*substantia et esse*]. ... On the other hand, in substances composed of matter and form there is a twofold composition of act and potentiality: the first of the substance itself which is composed of matter and form; the second, of the substance thus composed, and being [*esse*] ... It is therefore clear that composition of act and potentiality has greater extension than that of form and matter. Matter and form divide natural substance, while potentiality and act divide common being." *SCG II*, 54.

secures that God is the only being (*ens*) in which essence and existence are coexistent. Moreover, this doctrine gives Aquinas a way "to theorize as to how primary matter (the pure potentiality present in all material things) is entirely dependent ontologically upon the creative act of God (through the *esse* of its essential form, which gives existence to the materiality of the created substance)."[17] Creation—and by extension human essence—participates in existence only derivatively, as God gives existence to humankind. This human essence as it is the focus of Q75–Q86 of *Prima Pars* is composed of body and a soul. Here again one sees Aquinas's Christian dualism as dependent of the language of Chalcedon ("rational soul and body"). Although we cannot dive in here to hylomorphic theory and the relation of the soul as the form of the material body, for our purposes, we can simply defer to the affirmation that despite being intimately connected, the soul and the body are two different things.[18] We can further affirm that although the soul is individuated in matter by the body, both soul and body are necessary for human nature. Bodily existence is the proper state of humanity.

THESIS

The thesis of this book is that those who argue for the Son's assumption of a fallen human nature are mistaken because they invert trinitarian order, work with a faulty notion of the nature of the hypostatic union, or work with a defective notion of original sin. By retrieving the Patristic notion of inseparable operations, together with the Thomistic categories of grace of union and habitual grace, and the Post-Reformed theology of original sin, I will show that the formulations that assert that the Son assumed a fallen

---

17. White, *Wisdom in the Face of Modernity*, 83. There is some dispute on what Thomas really means when he asserts that Christ's humanity is a secondary *esse*. See Joshua Lee Gonnerman, "Substantial Act and Esse Secundarium: A Critique of Lonergan's 'Ontological and Psychological Constitution of Christ' " (Th.M., University of St. Michael's College Faculty of Theology and University of Toronto, 2012).

18. Ralph McInerny and John O'Callaghan write that "In 75.6, relying upon all that has gone before, Thomas argues that the human soul is a subsistent that is incorporeal, and thus does not cease to exist as a result of the death of the body. This result shows the soul to be a subsistent form that can exist without out matter." Ralph McInerny and John O'Callaghan, "Saint Thomas Aquinas," in *The Stanford Encyclopedia of Philosophy*, ed. Edward N. Zalta, Winter 2016 (Metaphysics Research Lab, Stanford University, 2016), https://plato.stanford.edu/archives/win2016/entries/aquinas/.

human nature are out of step with faithful, biblical, theological, and historical articulations. In order to explain this thesis further, I will summarize several of its main aspects: (1) what is meant by "inseparable operations," (2) what is meant by "Thomistic categories of grace of union and habitual grace," and (3) what is meant by "Post-Reformed theology of original sin."

INSEPARABLE OPERATIONS

The principle of *opera ad extra sunt indivisa* states that the works of the persons of the Trinity toward the outside are one.[19] They initiate in one and terminate in another person, following the order of God's inner modes of being. So, when sanctification is scripturally (1 Pet 1:2; Rom 8:13) and theologically tied to the Spirit, for example, it does not mean that his actions are separate from the other persons of the Trinity, but it means that the Spirit comes as the perfecter/finisher of something started by the Father and the Son. This is why the Spirit is usually connected to works of habit and progressive sanctification—because it most fits him to be the perfecter, or one who applies the works of Father and Son. Khaled Anatolios notes this pattern of trinitarian operation as he discusses Gregory of Nyssa's theology:

> [W]ith regard to the divine nature (*epi tes theias physeos*), we do not learn that the Father does something by himself, without the Son taking part [in that very action], nor again that the Son distinctly does something without the Spirit. Rather, every activity (*energeia*) reaching from God to creation and named according to our various conceptions (*ennoias*) originates in the Father, proceeds through the Son, and is completed in the Holy Spirit. The exertion of each in any act whatsoever is not separated and owned distinctly. But whatever happens in the course of the providence towards us or the management and constitution of the universe happens through the Three and yet does not result in three happenings.[20]

---

19. For a discussion of the Reformed Orthodox's reception of the doctrine of inseparable operations, see *PRRD* III, 257–63. For a dogmatic approach to this doctrine see John Webster, *God Without Measure: Working Papers in Christian Theology: Vol 1: God and the Works of God* (New York: Bloomsbury, T&T Clark, 2015), 162–64.

20. Khaled Anatolios, *Retrieving Nicaea: The Development and Meaning of Trinitarian Doctrine* (Grand Rapids: Baker Academic, 2011), 231.

The oneness of God's being forbids us to account for a separate work of each person in creation. This same unity, however, should not propel us to affirm an "undifferentiated agency in which the persons partake in exactly the same manner."[21] God's Trinitarian mode of agency, follows the order of his own being.[22] John Owen concludes: "The order of the subsistence of the persons in the same nature is represented unto us, and they have the same dependence on each other in their operations as they have in their subsistence."[23] Created order follows the same pattern of God's life in himself. Therefore in the incarnation, the Son's action precedes the action of the Spirit. Legge explains this reality in Thomistic fashion:

> The Son breathes forth the Spirit, not only eternally but also in his mission in the economy of grace. As the Son's eternal procession implies the procession of the Holy Spirit (the Father, in begetting his Son, gives the Son the power to spirate the Holy Spirit), so also the Son's visible mission intrinsically implies the Word breathing forth the Spirit to that same humanity. In eternity and in time, the Word proceeds from the Father, breathing forth Love. As Thomas explains elsewhere (with a quotation he attributes to Athanasius), "Christ himself as God the Son sent the Spirit from above, and as man below he received the Spirit; from himself to himself, therefore, the Spirit dwells in his humanity from his divinity."[24]

What Legge says here will have bearings for the next section; implying that habitual grace flows from grace of union. If we tie the work of the Spirit to habitual grace because of its perfecting character, then the most fitting kind of grace to be ascribed to the Son's assumption of his flesh is the grace of union.[25]

---

21. Anatolios asserts, "The notion of an altogether undifferentiated agency in which each of the persons partakes in exactly the same manner is also implicitly but very clearly ruled out by Gregory's consistent strategy of using three different verbs to distribute the common action distinctly to the three persons." Anatolios, *Retrieving Nicaea*, 231.

22. See Webster's discussion about *missiones sequuntur processiones*, in *God Without Measure*, 163.

23. *Works*, 4:92.

24. Dominic Legge, *The Trinitarian Christology of St Thomas Aquinas* (Oxford: Oxford University Press, 2017), 149.

25. John Owen also makes a similar point: "The Father is the fountain of all, as in being and existence, so in operation. The Son is of the Father, begotten of him, and, therefore, as

GRACE OF UNION AND HABITUAL GRACE

Thomas Aquinas correctly asserts that human nature stands in "need of the gratuitous will of God, in order to be lifted up to God."[26] However, the elevation of human nature up to God is twofold: (1) by operation—habitual— or (2) by personal being—grace of union. Aquinas's point is that both the sanctification of humankind and assumption of human nature by Christ are gracious sanctifying events. Nonetheless, the mode of elevation by operation is a habitual activity that is accidental. Contrary to the grace that unites human nature to the divine person, the accidental character of grace by operation results in a work that renders participation in likeness. The elevation by personal being, on the other hand, is greater because it is not accidental. The human nature is once and for all united to the person of the Son, not in a participation in likeness, but in a substantial union. Whereas, according to Aquinas, all saints participate in the operative grace, only Christ's human nature is *united* to the divine nature by grace of the person of the Son. The significance of this for the present work resides in the importance one places on the sanctification of Christ during his earthly ministry. If fallenness is a matter to be conquered in participation and sanctification like ours, then there might be a diminishing relevance to the hypostatic union—hence the importance of grace of union.

POST-REFORMED THEOLOGY OF ORIGINAL SIN

The era of the Reformed Orthodox was one of intense theological refinement. Richard Muller has argued extensively that there are continuities and discontinuities between the Reformers and the Reformed Orthodox.[27] Although there are many theological continuities, it is the contention of several scholars that original sin gained moderate revision during the period of the Protestant Scholastics. Calvin himself held to a semi-mediative view on the transmission of sin. For Calvin, it is metaphysically and

---

unto his work, is sent by him; but his own will is in and unto what he is sent about. The Holy Spirit proceedeth from the Father and the Son, and, therefore, is sent and given by them as to all the works which he immediately effecteth; but yet his own will is the direct principle of all that he doth,—he divideth unto every one according to his own will. And thus much may suffice to be spoken about the being of the Holy Spirit, and the order of his subsistence in the blessed Trinity." *Works*, 4:92.

26. *ST* III Q2. A10. co.

27. *PRRD* I, 37–40.

exegetically impossible to make the case that one is guilty of someone else's sin, but one still gets the corruption of his father, Adam.[28] The Protestant Scholastics, on the other hand, made a case that two things are present in the transmission of sin: corruption and guilt.

The important idea here is of the status of "public person" that Adam had. As Beeke and Jones said, "by the appointment of God, Adam and Christ were made public persons according to the covenants in which they represented their people, namely the covenant of works (Adam) and the covenant of redemption (Christ)."[29] The principal cue here is taken from a closer exegetical case in Romans 5.

There are both moral and legal status connected to the progeny of Adam due to his representativity. Reflecting on Romans 5 Owen states,

> [F]irst, in that his [Adam] voluntary act is imputed to us as ours, by reason of the covenant which was made with him on our behalf. But because this, consisting in an imputation, must needs be extrinsical unto us, therefore, secondly, we say that Adam, being the root and head of all human kind, and we all branches from that root, all parts of that body whereof he was the head, his will may be said to be ours. We were then all that one man,—we were all in him, and had no other will but his; so that though that be extrinsical unto us, considered as particular persons, yet it is intrinsical, as we are all parts of one common nature. As in him we sinned, so in him we had a will of sinning.[30]

In Owen's discussion we already see refinement upon Calvin's theology, for human nature is discussed with reference both to Adam's federal headship, and this external character of the theology of representation is included. The bearings of this for this work are crucial. For if Christ assumed a nature just like ours (post-lapsarian), guilt is necessarily connected to the progeny of Adam.

---

28. John Calvin, *Commentary on the Epistle to the Romans* (Grand Rapids: Baker Books, 1997), Romans 5:12.

29. Joel R. Beeke and Mark Jones, *A Puritan Theology: Doctrine for Life* (Grand Rapids: Reformation Heritage Books, 2012), 206.

30. *Works*, 10:73.

METHOD: DOGMATICS AND RETRIEVAL

Karl Barth starts his magisterial *Church Dogmatics* with a definition of dogmatics as "the scientific self-examination of the Christian church with respect to the content of its distinctive talk about God."[31] In this way, dogmatics is not disordered talk about God, but it is ordered thinking and talk in praise to the glory of the triune God of the gospel.

In ordering its thinking dogmatic theology first approaches topics from a necessary set of beliefs affirmed by a confessional group. As R. Lucas Stamps reminds us, dogmatics is not "mere articulation of a specific confessional symbol. Dogmatic theology does not merely describe what a particular church or denomination believes; it also seeks to defend what Christians *ought* to believe based on the authority of Scripture read in light of the Christian tradition."[32] Hence, even though there might not be a specific council on the issue of Christ's flesh, via relative ecumenical consensus and ecclesial implications, this dogmatic study is validated. Also, the eclectic group affirmed in the thesis (Roman Catholic, Patristic, and Post-Reformed theologies) presupposes an ecumenical account in this dogmatic approach.[33]

Second, retrieval in dogmatics means that "we inhabit the classroom of the communion of the saints and we seek to learn from their instruction."[34] This does not mean that retrieval in dogmatic theology is blind to the exegetical enterprise, but it means that while we appropriate the tradition, we do so critically. However, as Webster said, our attitude in retrieval is "much more trustful, more confident in the contemporary serviceability, unpersuaded by the superiority of the present age."[35] Scripture is held throughout this book as the *norma normans*, "the rule of rules." Tradition, nevertheless, will also hold an important place at the table, as it is the *norma normata*, "the ruled rule." Moreover, dogmatic reasoning (the wisdom of

---

31. *CD* I/1, 3.

32. Robert Lucas Stamps, "'Thy Will Be Done': A Dogmatic Defense of Dyothelitism in Light of Recent Monothelite Proposals" (PhD diss., The Southern Baptist Theological Seminary, 2014), 19.

33. Kevin Vanhoozer and Daniel Treier, *Theology and the Mirror of Scripture* (Downers Grove, IL: IVP Academic, 2015), 19–25.

34. Michael Allen and Scott Swain in "Introduction" by Michael Allen and Scott R. Swain, eds., *Christian Dogmatics: Reformed Theology for the Church Catholic* (Grand Rapids: Baker Academic, 2016), 4.

35. John Webster, "Theologies of Retrieval," in *The Oxford Handbook of Systematic Theology* ed. John Webster, Kathryn Tanner, and Iain R Torrance (New York: Oxford University Press, 2007), 592.

the church) comes from and sends one back to exegesis.[36] Dogmatics exists
in the retrieving mode for the sake of renewal—to help the church of the
Lord Jesus Christ respond to recent challenges with the wisdom from previous saints.

Since this work operates mainly from this dogmatic standpoint, it
draws from biblical, theological, and historical disciplines as the case
shall require, but in no particular priority. Both David Yeago and Kevin
Vanhoozer have argued that biblical theology is not actually closer to the
text than systematic or dogmatic theology. Yeago uses the idea of *concepts*
and *judgments* to articulate his point. For Yeago, one can use different concepts than the Bible to preserve the same judgments. Judgmental reality
is not an extraction of the textual concepts, but faithful judgments preserve the ideas of the biblical text by using different words.[37] Or, using
Vanhoozer's *theo-dramatic* model, one could say that Scripture is the script
and the acting is the living out of the text. As one improvises in acting to
different audiences, one is hopefully preserving the intention of the author,
while at the same time using different formats.[38] Therefore, because neither biblical, or systematic theologies are actually closer to the text than
the other, the eclectic pattern utilized in this dogmatic approach allows
for an interweaving of these disciplines as the case requires.

Chapter 2 not only deals with Karl Barth's theology of the *non-assumptus*,
but attempts to locate this subject in the entire project of reconciliation. In
order to do this, I discuss Barth's actualism and how that eventually places
Christ's history and essence in an interesting dialogue. Furthermore, his
theological project is set in the proper context of solidarity and grace. And
although actualism and solidarity could mean the attribution of fallenness
to the immanent life of God, Barth's project rejects this notion. The Son's
solidarity, however, deals with the sanctification of humanity. And the
hypostatic union continues and is guaranteed through Jesus's certainty
that the Father and his angels will hold and sanctify him in temptation.

---

36. Allen and Swain, *Christian Dogmatics*, 6.

37. D. S. Yeago, "The New Testament and the Nicene Dogma: A Contribution to the
Recovery of Theological Exegesis," *Sewanee Theological Review* 45, no. 4 (2002): 371–84.

38. Kevin Vanhoozer, "May We Go Beyond What is Written After All? The Pattern of
Theological Authority and the Problem of Doctrinal Development," in *The Enduring Authority
of the Christian Scriptures*, ed. D. A. Carson (Grand Rapids: Eerdmans, 2016), 760.

Chapter 3 deals with T. F. Torrance. For Torrance, a few intuitions guide the atonement. The first is a response to what he calls the "Latin heresy," in which the work of Christ in the cross is analyzed separately from his life as God the Son incarnate. Therefore, creating all sorts of problems such as legal fiction and externality of the gospel. The second, and a consequence of the first, is that in order to fully heal human nature Christ had to take upon himself a fallen human nature.

Torrance's formulation of the fallen human nature is dependent upon his rejection of the Latin heresy. Christ had to be united to all humanity and redeem it from the inside of his personal union. My goal, however, is to show that such a position is at least unstable because it depends upon a questionable philosophical view of human nature. Also, on a deeper level, Torrance's defense of the *non-assumptus* is problematic because it is never clear when the personal union is complete. If Christ heals humanity within his inner constitution and redeems humanity in himself, then is the hypostatic union conjoined during the incarnation, but only united after the resurrection? To achieve this goal, I will describe Torrance's rejection of the Latin heresy in terms of his advance of the doctrine of "theosis." Once I have shown that he is rejecting any "external" concept of the atonement, I focus on his most problematic rejection of the Latin heresy—*via* his formulation of the fallen humanity of Christ (*non-assumptus*). In this last section, I focus the problem of the virgin birth.

Chapter 4 starts the constructive part of the book. After surveying some initial articulations and developments of the doctrine of inseparable operations, most of the argument will build on scholastic distinctions of real relations, missions and acts, and visible and invisible missions. Such distinctions allow one to understand what exactly "assuming" mean. To assume is not simply "to get," but presupposes (if one follows the scholastic distinctions) both passivity and activity. After these notions have been established, then Barth and Torrance's projects will be evaluated. Needless to say, such evaluation is only possible once Torrance and Barth have been already understood under their own rubrics in the previous chapters. In these new chapters, the twentieth-century theologians will be checked "against" the western and scholastic tradition. Sometimes, they reject these formulations and the tradition entirely and try to construct a metaphysical scheme on their own (i.e., Barth's actualism), but the assumption of human nature cannot be a totally independent doctrine. Certainly, the incarnation is a mystery, but even as a mystery, the incarnation is not isolated in history. The two metaphysical schemes have to be judged upon Scripture and reason.

Chapter 5 discusses the relationship of grace and nature as they relate to the incarnation. The entry point into this section will be the somewhat recent Roman Catholic kerfuffle over the existence of pure nature. In a dialogue with Herman Bavinck, I will argue that although Bavinck's conception that grace is only opposed to sin and not nature is correct, some scholastic distinctions on the relationship of grace and nature in the incarnation are helpful. Here, I will appeal to grace of union and habitual grace. Through a robust notion of how the Son's human nature is actually sanctified, one can avoid the errors of those who propose Christ's assumption of a fallen nature. In a way, this chapter is borrowing some conceptual apparatus from chapter four. Since it will be made clear that created reality does not contradict God's inner order, then I will argue that proposing an assumption of fallen nature needs to suppose that habitual grace is occurring "before" the actual personal union.

Chapter 6 is on the doctrine of original sin. Although the doctrine has major developments in the early church, the focus of this chapter will be on Calvin and developments of the doctrine of original sin after the Swiss Reformer. After discussing a recent interpretation of Calvin's doctrine of original sin, I will try to propose a *via media* between this recent interpreter and some other established scholars. Nonetheless, Calvin's doctrine still needed some development and again, with the assistance of Herman Bavinck's organic motif, I will show how federal headship avoids not only the charge of arbitrariness in the transmission of sin, but also avoids the assumption of a fallen nature in Christ.

At the conclusion I revisit each chapter with hopes to clarify that asserting that the Son assumed a fallen human nature does not pay close attention to the Trinitarian nature of the act of assumption, nor does it carefully work through the metaphysics of grace—especially in its Thomistic form—nor does it judicially conceptualize the biblical pattern of representation regarding original sin.

SCHOLARLY CONTRIBUTIONS, JUSTIFICATION, AND THE NATURE OF THIS STUDY

Much of the discussion regarding the *non-assumptus* goes back to claims from the early church fathers. Although John Romanides, the late long-time editor of *The Greek Orthodox Theological Review,* believed that the fathers universally held to a notion of Christ's assumption of an Adamic-like nature,[39] T. F. Torrance believed that several fathers were on the side of the *non-assumptus.*[40] Although there is a legitimate debate over the position of the fathers (Greek and Latin), this study will not discuss this quarrel at length (even if at times it will touch on it). While this book will mention certain debates, the main interlocutors will be Karl Barth and T. F. Torrance. The reason for this choice is because both move past some of the shortcomings of Irving and also because recent developments in the doctrine often appeal to their dogmatic (in Barth's case) and retrieval (in Torrance's case) work. Moreover, the task of arbitrating the appropriation of the church fathers has recently been taken up in E. Jerome van Kuiken's published dissertation.[41] In van Kuiken's monograph, he surveys ten church fathers and ten modern proponents of the *non-assumptus* and the unfallen position. His main goal was to first, determine "the degree of accuracy in modern debaters' handling of Christian tradition; and secondly, to exploit any patristic insights which may contribute towards resolving the current debate."[42] I have already pointed to this elsewhere saying,

> van Kuiken carefully looks into both the Greek and Latin church fathers. Although some Greek Fathers—for example, Gregory of Nyssa—might be more favorable to the language of a fallen or sinful humanity, no exact parallel can be found in Latin Christology. The

---

39. Romanides asserts, "The teaching of Julian of Halicarnassus that the Logos united to Himself manhood as it was before the fall is not in itself wrong and is accepted by all Fathers. What is wrong with Julian's position, as pointed out by Father Samuel, is that the human nature of Christ was considered incorruptible before the resurrection." J. Romanides, "Unofficial Consultation between Theologians of Eastern Orthodox and Oriental Orthodox Churches, August 11–15, 1964: Papers and Minutes," *The Greek Orthodox Theological Review* 10, no. 2 (1964): 7–160.

40. Thomas F. Torrance, *The Trinitarian Faith: The Evangelical Theology of the Ancient Catholic Church* (Edinburgh: T&T. Clark, 1988).

41. Van Kuiken, *Christ's Humanity in Current and Ancient Controversy: Fallen or Not?*

42. Ibid., 2.

main christological parallel might be the virginal conception in which "God's Son breaks the hold of sin upon human nature so that his own humanity, like unfallen Adam's, is unblemished by sin, uncontrolled by Satan, and under no debt to die."[43]

Regardless of the conclusion van Kuiken reaches, my main goal is to lay out fences regarding talk about the fallen view. Thus, even though van Kuiken's dissertation is a major accomplishment, the uniqueness of my work lies in the positive construction of a model to reject the fallen view.

Other major studies have been published on the *non-assumptus*. Some have engaged this task trying to build upon Barth and Torrance—exegetically, theologically, and historically.[44] Other works have engaged with the *non-assumptus* in more polemical manner. Some try to defend[45] Barth and Torrance; others try to refute them in this particular doctrine.[46] Some recent studies have been published on the humanity of Christ in the thought of T. F. Torrance by trying to further some ethical implications of the *non-assumptus*,[47] while others, even though not so dependent upon the *non-assumptus* per se, have used it as a proxy to get at other main theological propositions.[48] Finally, some in the realm of analytic theology have taken upon themselves to evaluate the doctrine of the *non-assumptus* in

---

43. Rafael Bello, review of *Christ's Humanity in Current and Ancient Controversy: Fallen or Not?* by E. Jerome van Kuiken, Reading Religion, accessed November 17, 2018. http://readingreligion.org/books/christs-humanity-current-and-ancient-controversy.

44. See Harry Johnson, *The Humanity of the Saviour: A Biblical and Historical Study of the Human Nature of Christ in Relation to Original Sin, with Special Reference to Its Soteriological Significance* (London: Epworth, 1962), 193, and Thomas G Weinandy, *In the Likeness of Sinful Flesh: An Essay on the Humanity of Christ* (Edinburgh: T&T Clark, 1993).

45. Christian D. Kettler, "The Vicarious Humanity of Christ and the Reality of Salvation" (Ph.D. diss., Fuller Theological Seminary, 1986).

46. Kevin Chiarot, *The Unassumed Is the Unhealed: The Humanity of Christ in the Theology of T. F. Torrance* (Eugene, OR: Pickwick, 2013), 21. See also William Duncan Rankin, "Carnal Union with Christ in the Theology of T. F. Torrance" (PhD diss., The University of Edinburgh, 1997), and Emmanuel Hatzidakis, *Jesus: Fallen? The Human Nature of Christ Examined from an Eastern Orthodox Perspective by Emmanuel Hatzidakis* (Clearwater, FL: Orthodox Witness, 2013), 25.

47. See Todd Speidell, *Fully Human in Christ: The Incarnation as the End of Christian Ethics* (Eugene, OR: Wipf and Stock, 2016), 6, and Myk Habets Habets, *Theosis in the Theology of Thomas Torrance* (Farnham, England: Ashgate, 2009), 82.

48. R. Michael Allen, *The Christ's Faith: A Dogmatic Account* (New York: Bloomsbury T&T Clark, 2009).

its inner logic. While some analytic theologians have seen the doctrine as logically coherent, that conclusion is not a consensus.[49]

A widely refenced article is Kelly Kapic's "The Son's Assumption of a Human Nature: A Call for Clarity." Here, Kapic does not necessarily argue for one position, but he attempts to survey what are the main claims of each position and demonstrate that there are miscommunications in the debate. For example, discussing the Reformation era, Kapic states that "a few samples will suffice to demonstrate that the inheritance of original sin is commonly thought equivalent to claiming one is a sinner."[50] Depending, however, on how one treats the communication of original sin, Kapic explains that corruption may not be understood as moral. After this survey, Kapic writes some observations of what is some common ground between fallen and unfallen advocates. These observations are worthy to be reproduced at length here:

> First, both fallen and unfallen adherents oppose those who have treated Mary simply as a "channel," affirming rather that the Son is able from Mary to assume a complete human nature: including a reasonable soul (with all its various faculties) and physical body. Second, both positions affirm that the incarnate Son of God entered not a pre-fallen paradise. Third, all sides of the debate recognize that the Holy Spirit is active in rendering Christ "without sin." Fourth, fallen and unfallen position say that the temptations of Christ are real. Kapic also raises a few interesting questions that need to be clarified in the debate. For example, do supporters of the *non-assumptus* endorse concupiscence in the human nature of Christ? And what is the relationship between original sin and guilt?[51]

Other works engage with this doctrine. However, due to the limited scope of this work and the dialogue partners chosen, discussion of these works will either be present in the body of the book—as these authors

---

49. See Ian A. McFarland, "Fallen or Unfallen? Christ's Human Nature and the Ontology of Human Sinfulness," *IJST* 10, no. 4 (October 2008): 412; Rolfe King, "Assumption, Union and Sanctification: Some Clarifying Distinctions," *IJST* 19, no. 1 (November 2016): 53–72; and Oliver Crisp, "Did Christ Have a Fallen Human Nature?," *IJST* 6, no. 3 (July 2004): 270–88.

50. Kelly M. Kapic, "The Son's Assumption of a Human Nature: A Call for Clarity," *IJST* 3, no. 2 (July 2001): 154–66.

51. Kapic, "The Son's Assumption of a Human Nature," 64–66.

develop the thought of Barth and Torrance—or they will be pointed out for future studies.[52]

The great array of opinions and theological approaches open space for a fresh look at the theology of the *non-assumptus*. This work attempts to clarify the talk about the humanity of Christ, by providing Trinitarian, Thomistic and Post-Reformation categories that create a kind of fence for talk about the moral status of the humanity of the savior.

WHAT DO THESE TERMS MEAN?
ASSUMPTION AND FALLEN/UNFALLEN:
A TENTATIVE CLARIFICATION APPROACH

One of the contributions made by E. Jerome Van Kuiken was to, after surveying roughly twenty scholars, attempt some terminological clarity. It becomes clear from the beginning of the debate regarding Christ's human flesh in the twentieth century that terms like "sinful," "fallen," "affected," and others can take a great range of meaning depending of who is treating them.

For example, van Kuiken points that the term "assumed" is used to describe the "condition *out of which* he assumed it or the condition *into which* he assumed."[53] According to van Kuiken, whereas those who think Christ had a fallen human nature would like to emphasize the latter, those who think Christ assumed an unfallen human nature would prefer the former. In any case, the simple statement that Christ assumed a fallen or depraved nature could be accepted by those defending the unfallen side of

---

52. For examples of the fruitful debate, see Ho-Jin Ahn, "The Humanity of Christ: John Calvin's Understanding of Christ's Vicarious Humanity," *SJT* 65, no. 2 (2012): 145–58; Allen, "Calvin's Christ"; Ivor J. Davidson, "Pondering the Sinlessness of Jesus Christ: Moral Christologies and the Witness of Scripture," *IJST* 10, no. 4 (October 1, 2008): 372–98; Daniel J. Cameron and Myk Habets, *Flesh and Blood: A Dogmatic Sketch Concerning the Fallen Nature View of Christ's Human Nature* (Eugene, OR: Wipf and Stock, 2016); John Clark and Marcus Peter Johnson, *The Incarnation of God: The Mystery of the Gospel as the Foundation of Evangelical Theology* (Wheaton, IL: Crossway, 2015); Bruce L. McCormack, "For Us and Our Salvation: Incarnation and Atonement in the Reformed Tradition," *The Greek Orthodox Theological Review* 43, no. 1/4 (1998): 281–316; Marilyn McCord Adams, *What Sort of Human Nature?: Medieval Philosophy and the Systematics of Christology* (Milwaukee: Marquette University, 1999); Kapic, "The Son's Assumption of a Human Nature," 154–66; Stoyan Tanev, "The Concept of Energy in T. F. Torrance and in Orthodox Theology," *Participatio: Journal of the Thomas F. Torrance Theological Fellowship* 4, no. 1 (2013): 190–212; Crisp, *Divinity and Humanity*.

53. Van Kuiken, *Christ's Humanity in Current and Ancient Controversy*, 167.

the debate, insofar as that simply means that is the condition *out of which* he assumed (the only theologians for whom this could cause any problems are those defending the immaculate conception).[54] The problem with van Kuiken's proposal is that like many theological terms, treating "assumed" in this manner is to proclaim the term's death *via* too many qualifications.

As I argue in the chapter on inseparable operations, Thomas and the scholastic tradition provided a way forward in the debate by defining what is an act. The term assumed has to be seen in its proper Trinitarian structure. As Vidu states, "Trinitarian persons act as a single agent in the economy, such that each Trinitarian person is co-agent in each other's action tokens."[55] This means that even though it is only the Son who is incarnate, the act of assuming is caused by all three persons of the Trinity because "each is co-agent in each other's action tokens."[56] An action is not only a *state*. Each Trinitarian person is involved in the action of the assumption of human nature, because each person caused it. The *state*, however, resulted from this action is only appropriate to the Son. By resorting to this Thomistic approach, I hope that it may be clear that any fallen proposal could eventually lend a hand to the idea that the persons of the Trinity are causing the assumption of sin.

Terms like "unfallen" and "fallen" also carry a certain baggage. The idea that Christ has an unfallen human nature is usually tied to the concept of a pre-lapsarian human nature. Van Kuiken, however, reminded us that such talk can be interpreted as if Jesus was never even affected by the fall or that his humanity existed before the fall. Although such reading is at times uncharitable, the point is, according to van Kuiken, that "unfallen" communicates a perfectionism that should be avoided. A suggestion was

---

54. Van Kuiken, *Christ's Humanity in Current and Ancient Controversy*, 167.

55. Adonis Vidu, "Trinitarian Inseparable Operations and the Incarnation," *Journal of Analytic Theology* 4, no. 1 (2016): 106.

56. Again, Vidu states, "From an action perspective, the agency in the case of the incarnation/assumption belongs to the Trinity as a whole. Father, Son, and Holy Spirit are together causing the assumption. In other words, they are together bringing it about that a relationship of dependence obtains between this human nature and the person of the Son. However, from a state perspective, it is said that the action terminates on the Son. In other words, from a state perspective the action results in a state that characterizes the Son alone. Thus, Augustine's "reference to a single person" means that in this particular case, the human flesh is really united and made dependent on the person of the Logos." Ibid., 113.

made, then, for the replacement of "unfallen" with "restored."[57] This would
yield a dynamism lacking in the unfallen terminology.[58] McCormack states,

> On this view the question posed at the outset—was Christ's human
> nature fallen or Unfallen—cannot be answered without qualifi-
> cation. It was indeed a fallen human nature in that it was taken
> from the substance of sinful human flesh. But it was made to be
> "unfallen"—or better, a "restored" true humanity, for this was in
> the strictest sense not a new creation—by the sanctifying work of
> the Spirit.[59]

McCormack is correct. Christ does draw his humanity from Mary, who
is a sinner. The idea of sanctification, however, needs to be qualified as well.
The sanctification occurred in the Son's assumption of human nature is
both unlike and like the sanctification of humankind. It is unlike because
the grace of union resulted from the incarnation can only be given to
that particular human nature. It is like other humankind's sanctification
because the Spirit also dwells in Christ, sanctifying his humanity in *habitus* fashion. Giving up on the term unfallen has noble motives, but it can
generate more questions than answers. In the end, if one choses "restored"
we might also have to spend time qualifying the mode of sanctification.

Let us take stock of the approach presented here: "Assumed" cannot
be seen as an isolated operation of the Son, but it demands a Trinitarian
framework. Furthermore, the "fallen"/"unfallen" terminology should not
be discarded because it may tend to static notions of the incarnation. Any
direction one goes, the perils of clarification *ad nauseam* are present. So,
keeping with classically used terms, as long as they have their Trinitarian
framework as foundation this will aid one's analysis.

---

57. McCormack, "For Us and Our Salvation," 296.
58. Ibid.
59. Ibid.

2

KARL BARTH'S THEOLOGY OF THE INCARNATION AND CHRIST'S FLESH

The number of resources dealing with Karl Barth's (1886–1968) doctrine of the incarnation in recent years has grown exponentially.[1] Though the Swiss theologian is often quoted as one of the proponents of the doctrine of the *non-assumptus,* no monograph has been produced dedicated exclusively to Barth's reception and/or formulation of this doctrine. Although the fallen human nature of Christ plays a central role for T. F. Torrance's doctrines of the incarnation and atonement,[2] Barth's treatment of this doctrine has been marginalized.

Barth discusses the Son's assumption of a fallen state in *Church Dogmatics* IV/1, under §59, "The Obedience of the Son of God." In this section, Barth is at pains to show that the Son is *pro nobis.* Embedded into the *pro nobis* character of the atonement for sins is the person of Jesus Christ.

---

1. Darren O. Sumner, "The Twofold Life of the Word: Karl Barth's Critical Reception of the Extra Calvinisticum," *IJST* 15, no. 1 (January 2013): 42–57; Darren O. Sumner, *Karl Barth and the Incarnation: Christology and the Humility of God,* T&T Clark Studies in Systematic Theology. (London: Bloomsbury, 2014); Paul D. Jones, *The Humanity of Christ: Christology in Karl Barth's Church Dogmatics,* T&T Clark Theology (New York: T&T Clark, 2008); Thomas Joseph White, *The Incarnate Lord: A Thomistic Study in Christology* (Washington, DC: The Catholic University of America Press, 2016),] 1, 2; Rustin E. Brian, *Covering Up Luther: How Barth's Christology Challenged the Deus Absconditus That Haunts Modernity* (Eugene, OR: Cascade Books, 2013); Edwin Chr Van Driel, *Incarnation Anyway: Arguments for Supralapsarian Christology* (Oxford: Oxford University Press, 2008). David Gibson, *Reading the Decree: Exegesis, Election and Christology in Calvin and Barth,* T&T Clark Studies in Systematic Theology (New York: T&T Clark, 2009); Adam Neder, *Participation in Christ: An Entry into Karl Barth's Church Dogmatics* (Louisville, KY: Westminster John Knox Press, 2009).

2. Torrance even received entire monographs dealing with the *non-assumptus.* Kevin Chiarot, *The Unassumed Is the Unhealed: The Humanity of Christ in the Christology of T. F. Torrance* (Eugene:OR, Pickwick, 2013).

Christ is in solidarity with humankind. Such solidarity is not merely external or forensic in character but is who the Son of God is in the far country.
Solidarity is Christ's identification with humankind in his humility and
in humanity's exaltation.

I intend to look into two sections of *CD* IV/1 and another from *CD* IV/2
where Barth affirms the *non-assumptus*. I will also exegete another commonly appealed section from *CD* I/2 (under §15—Barth's early construction
of the doctrine). I will argue that despite Barth's pastoral and ethical concerns for the affirmation of the *non-assumptus*,[3] there are some problems
that the doctrine of the fallen human flesh and the sinlessness of Christ
pose for the hypostatic union.[4] These problems are further articulated in
his doctrine of the *communicatio gratiarum* in which the communication of
graces to the human nature as discussed by Barth, may divide the natures
and thereby suggest an implicit Nestorianism. I am not arguing that Karl
Barth was Nestorian, but that maybe his doctrine of the *communicatio gratiarum*, used to protect the Son from sin, may have unintentionally separated the natures in a Nestorian direction.

This study will progress in six steps. First, I will set Barth's discussion in what he sees are the historical and theological backgrounds of his
"re-discovery" of the *non-assumptus*. Second, I will explain Barth's understanding of the self-humiliation of the Son in light of the event of Jesus
Christ's solidarity with us. Third, I will discuss the issue of sinlessness
and the antecedent life of the Son as it relates to the fallen state of Christ
and the grace of God in the incarnation. Fourth, I will evaluate those proposals in light of Karl Barth's doctrine of the *communicatio gratiarum*. Fifth,
I will identify some recent contributions that try to retrieve Barth's formulation in order to argue for the fallen flesh of Christ. Finally, with the
aid of Thomas Aquinas's categories of grace of union and habitual grace,
I will propose a mild and brief evaluative-corrective to Barth's doctrine of
the *non-assumptus* and impeccability based on a few perceived missteps
in Barth's formulation.

---

3. *CD* IV/1, 216.
4. *CD* IV/1, 258–59.

EARLY STAGES OF ARGUMENTATION:
FLESH AND IDENTITY

In §15, Barth discusses the "Mystery of Revelation." Under this rubric, he talks about the assumption, sanctification, and existence of the Word with us and Godself. He sets the stage by asserting that "very God and very man" are unnegotiable aspects to true christological speech. Nonetheless, there is a proper order that needs to be maintained: since he never ceases to be very God when assuming human nature, we have to start by protecting the divine aspect of our christological discourses.[5]

Once Barth has protected the divine person, he then discusses what does it mean for the Word to become flesh. The unity of flesh in the person of the Son should prompt us to have no reservation in ascribing to the humanity of Christ the revelation of "God Himself in person."[6] For Barth, the humanity of Christ is the revelation of the eternal Word in such a way that even the name *Logos* is merely seen as a placeholder for Jesus Christ.[7]

Flesh, however, does not mean a mere human being. Flesh for Barth implies an "essence and existence" which makes a human a human as opposed to God, angel, or animal.[8] The primary meaning then for "The Word became flesh" is that the Word became participant in human essence and existence. Nonetheless, this can only be real in the concrete life of the person Jesus Christ. Barth's movement here avoids at once adoptionists tendencies by maintaining in check the *an-en-hypostatic* theology (he appeals to Wollebius, "*Christus non hominem, sed humanitatem, non personam sed naturam assumit*"[9]). The essence and existence of this person was never a reality of itself, but according to Barth because the Son became this person the possibility of that human nature came into being in him. Moreover, Barth asserts that in this assumption the Word and human were not really side by side (therefore formally rejecting Nestorianism). This human exists because "the Son of God appropriated and actualized His

---

5. *CD* I/2, 136. Here he cites Epiphanius as support for the irreversibility of the statement. "very God and very man."

6. *CD* I/2, 148.

7. See Rafael Bello, Review of "Reading the Gospels with Karl Barth," *Reading Religion*, accessed February 22, 2018, http://readingreligion.org/books/reading-gospels-karl-barth.

8. Here Barth appeals to Polanus's *Natura human Christi est essential seu substantia humana, qua Christus nobis hominibus coessentialis est. CD* I/2,149.

9. *CD* I/2,

special possibility as a Man. ... this is the sole ground of existence, of this
Man, and therefore of Christ's flesh."[10] The strong unity that Barth references here is explained in terms of identifying the reality of Jesus Christ
"as God Himself in person actively present in the flesh."[11] Hence, the human
Jesus Christ is Himself God in the flesh—not a demigod, nor an ideal human,
but God's Word in person who represents us to God and God to us.[12]

Next, Barth is concerned to debunk any view in which σάρξ describes
a neutral human nature. Since σάρξ, in the New Testament, concerns not
only humankind in general but the situation in which humankind is liable
to judgement and verdict of God—under His wrath. Σάρξ is the "concrete
form of human nature marked by Adam's fall."[13] Hence, the identity of
the Son of Man is bound up with a post-lapsarian human nature. Since
Barth has already established that this unity is not fictitious but real—for
the humanity of Christ is the revelation of Godself—it would be natural
to identify this move with sin in the divine life. I should note however,
Barth's careful initial move in this section when he asserts that "very God
and very man" have a proper order. We hold to the unity of the person, but
we protect the divinity of the Godhead.

Once divinity is protected and identity with the post fall is asserted,
Barth continues discussing that the identity of the Word with post-fall
flesh is not only external, but like ours even in our opposition to him.[14] This
movement is the greatest inconceivable but true revelatory one—that He
is God's revelation to us; he would not be revelation if he was not a human
being, and he would not be a human being if he was not σάρξ in this definite sense.

Becoming σάρξ in this definite sense, however, does not mean that he
was a sinful man.[15] He entered into solidarity (according to Barth, internally
and externally—whatever it means) with us. Only by bearing *innocently*

---

10. *CD* I/2, 150.

11. *CD* I/2, 151.

12. Paul Dafydd Jones has argued convincingly that the *an-en-hypostatic* pair serves as
a theologumenon that mediates Barth's critical realism and his dogmatic appropriation of
sixteenth-century dogmatics in its dialectic fashion Jones, *The Humanity of Christ*, 23.

13. *CD* I/2, 151.

14. *CD* I/2,

15. *CD* I/2, 152.

what Adam and we are guilty of doing can he reveal God to us. Barth takes his cues from Hebrews 2:18; 4:15; and 5:2. These classic texts are commonly associated with the compassion of the Son for our humanity. Nonetheless, Barth seems to take it a step further. If to say that to become flesh is simply to become human or even a hero, we descend to the level of other religions. Christ's compassion extends to the fact that he "became sin." No other religion affirms such a thing.

The early moves from *CD* I/2 regarding the *non-assumptus* are still situated in Barth's theology of identification, but with a lower actualistic force. Following Bruce McCormack's interpretation, it is possible to locate a heightened mode of speech regarding the identity of the Son in the Godhead as the man Jesus after *CD* I/2. As I will show, even though the actualism plays its part in Barth's construal, it is not determinative to attribute fallenness in the Godhead. Paul Dafydd Jones has located a second actualistic move that makes sense of the incarnation *via* the pairing of the *en-an-hypostasia* and the *communicatio naturarum.* Jones states,

> McCormack's interpretation can be intensified and tightened up somewhat. The key point is this: Barth's actualism encompasses not only Christ's human relation to the Father but also the relation of the assumed human to the divine Son. Although the man Jesus lacks his own *hypostasis* (a non-essential property of human being), he does not lack agential power (an essential property of human being), and he exerts this power in a way that contributes to, and in fact assists in the establishment and preservation of, the personal simplicity definitive of his divine-human person. Specifically, the word "participation," while sidestepping the problematic insinuation of an interpenetrative co-inherence of "natures," allows Barth to suggest that the union of humanity and divinity in Christ's person is an event mutually confected and, in some respect, mutually forged, given the concurrent activity of Christ's humanity and Christ's divinity. While unilaterally established, this union is neither unilaterally imposed nor unilaterally sustained. Each essence "takes part" in the task of upholding the numerical simplicity of Christ's person; "on both sides there is a true and genuine participation" (IV/2, page 62). *Pace* McCormack, it is not quite that one essence is

particularly involved in "receiving" and the other essence is particularly involved in "giving." Rather, Christ's essences together
enact and realize Christ's personally simple identity. On the one
side, the divine act of incarnation fulfills God's decision to be the
"electing God." God realizes, under the conditions of time and space,
the utterly particular identity that God pre-temporally assigns to
the divine Son. The divine Son is therefore the subject who directs
and animates comprehensively the person of Christ; the divine Son
is the "who" of Christ's person. On the other side, Christ *qua* human
is given, receives and then acts to affirm and uphold the simple
identity definitive of his person. Christ's human essence does its
"bit" to ensure that Christ is the person that God wills him to be and
that he is—the Word incarnate.[16]

Jones's intuitions here seem correct. Dogmatic retrieval made it possible for Barth to eventually stop seeing the incarnation in control of the
divine consortium. Eventually, as we move from *CD* I/2 to *CD* IV/1 and *CD*
IV/2 these convictions are more settled and the *vere deus et vere homo* start
to be mutually determinative. So we move now (after the *excursus*) to *CD*
IV in hopes to trace Barth's reasoning of identity and flesh as it relates to
his mature Christology.

EXCURSUS: GLEANINGS FROM THE HISTORY OF THE CHURCH IN *CHURCH DOGMATICS*

Since the early church, theology has been diverted from its proper course
(even if this course was well-intentionally diverted). Barth announced
that in an effort to protect the impeccability of Jesus, the church softened
its declaration of the kind of flesh Jesus assumed: "But there must be no
weakening or obscuring of the saving truth that the nature which God
assumed is identical with our nature as we see it in the light of the fall. If
it was otherwise how could Christ be like us?"[17] With solidarity, the Son
who was without sin was made sin. Hence, Barth asserts that we must
disagree with Gregory of Nyssa who posited that since God is good and

---

16. Jones, *The Humanity of Christ*, 133.
17. CD I/2, 153.

good cannot cohabitate with sin, the incarnation is in accordance with the intrinsic goodness of creation.[18] We cannot agree with Honorius also, who said "*a divinitate assumpta est nostra natura, non culpa, illa (natura) profecto, quae ante peccatum creata est, non quae post praevaricationem vitiate.*"[19] Barth's simple response in light of his own theology of solidarity is that his is *natura vitiata.*

Barth also points to Calvin, the Leiden Synopsis, Luther, and Hollaz as guilty of weakening the truth that the flesh the Son assumed was one like ours and also of neglecting texts like 2 Corinthians 5:21 and Galatians 3:13.[20] The Leiden Synopsis (with its scholastic tendencies) weakened the theological point even more. The Synopsis says in Disputation 25.18: "for it is not fitting that human nature guilty of sin be united to the Son of God" (*non enim conveniebat humanam naturam peccatum obnoxiam Filio Dei uniri*). Barth thinks that if it is not fitting (*conveniebat*) for the Son to take a nature like ours, it is impossible for him to represent us. Moreover, although there is a laudable desire to protect God's honor, this movement also rejects the scriptural exaltation that happens in condescension.[21]

Nonetheless, there have been a few enlightened figures in history. He cites Gottfried Menken, Edward Irving, J. C. von Hoffman, H. F. Kohlbrügge, Edward Bohl, and H. Bezzel as the few who were courageous to stand against the tradition's wish to protect the honor of God, but that at the same time compromised his condescending empathy.

Some of the movements exemplified in the figures above resemble Barth's talk of solidarity. Others take it further (with Barth's blessings). Such is the case of Edward Irving who asserts that the sinlessness of Christ

---

18. Or. Cat. 15.

19. Honorius I Denz No. 251.

20. *CD* I/2, 153. The first translation of the Leiden Synopsis has just been published in English and it is an excellent work. See Henk Van Den Belt et al: *Synopsis Purioris Theologiae / Synopsis of Purer Theology: Latin Text and English Translation*, Lam edition (Leiden ; Boston: Brill Academic, 2016); Dolf te Velde et al., eds., *Synopsis Purioris Theologiae / Synopsis of a Purer Theology: Latin Text and English Translation: Disputations 1–23*, bilingual ed. (Leiden: Brill Academic Pub, 2014).

21. The relationship of exaltation and humiliation shall be taken at a later stage in this book. For now, it suffices to say that Barth thinks they are simultaneous. See Rob Price's superb published dissertation: Robert B. Price, *Letters of the Divine Word: The Perfections of God in Karl Barth's Church Dogmatics* (New York: T&T Clark, 2011). See also Jeremy R. Treat, *The Crucified King: Atonement and Kingdom in Biblical and Systematic Theology* (Grand Rapids: Zondervan, 2014), 156–64.

is not in virtue of the presence of the divine person of the Son who sanctifies it but due to the presence of the Holy Spirit. For Irving, since Christ
assumed a manhood that was fallen, he needed to experience the grace/
favor of God in overcoming sin. Barth quotes Irving saying that "Christ
was holy in spite of the law of the flesh working in Him as in another
man; but never in Him prevailing."[22] We will take Barth's articulation of
the sinlessness of Christ below; it seems, however, that he is taking his
cues from Irving. Although Barth does not discuss the role of the Spirit
in keeping Christ sinless; his move is similar to Irving's. In *CD* IV/1, Barth
will connect sinlessness with the giving of grace. It is to that movement
that we turn now.

DEUS PRO NOBIS

Engraved in *CD* IV/1, 211–217 is Barth's preoccupation with solidarity in
the humility of the Son. "God has not abandoned the world and man in
the unlimited need of his situation, but He willed to bear the need as his
own."[23] Salvation is not an external act of the triune God in favor of man,
but "He humbles Himself to our status in order to be our companion in that
status … in order to change the status from within."[24] This act of humility
is probably the rationale for Barth's alignment of fallen human nature with
Christ. No doubt there is a very good intuition operating here. Solidarity
is a central biblical concept in the atonement and here Barth's actualistic
theology harmonizes even better with the theme of solidarity. It is not
solidarity from the incarnation forward. It is solidarity from the "history
in which He is God."[25]

For Barth, "We explain the incarnation docetically and therefore
explaining it away, we should be closing our eyes … the Word became flesh
means that the Son made his own the situation of man."[26] The Son is not
only in solidarity with humankind in eternity (*via* divine humility), but
also in time one must explain the incarnation as one in which the Son

---

22. *CD* I/2, 154.

23. *CD* IV/1, 215.

24. *CD* IV/1, 216.The self-humiliation of the Son of God, according to Barth in §59, is never
an isolated theologoumenon, but is always accompanied by the exaltation of man.

25. *CD* IV/1, 203.

26. *CD* IV/1, 215–16.

takes fallen flesh, otherwise one falls into docetism. Docetism is the christological heresy Barth rejects in his formulation of the assumption of the fallen flesh of Christ—Jesus does not merely appear to be fully human— He is fully human. So, Barth equates being fully human with a fallen state of flesh. The most important questions here are what is a human nature? What is needed for the Son's assumption of human nature in order for him to be in solidarity with humankind? Is sin a necessary property of human nature?[27] It is hard to find an answer to these questions, especially considering Barth's uneasiness with the vocabulary of Chalcedon at times. Even raising these questions does not seem like the natural flow of Barth's argument. As said before, Barth's main concern here is solidarity. Humankind is not alone; they were not left with sin and its own devices. What is clear from this passage (even if that is not Barth's main preoccupation) is that he prefers a maximalist account of humanity in which sin is not an independent ontological entity that takes hold of humankind but is essential to humankind's composition to be human after Adam.[28]

In fact, sin is more than necessary for human nature *per se*. For Barth, sin must be addressed christologically (not Adamically). Just as no theological *loci* has an independent status, so hamartiology has no other foundation but Christ.[29] As Tseng puts it, for Barth, "to consider sin independently of Christ as such is to give sin an ontological status alongside God, thus turning sin into a second god."

In §60 "The Pride and Fall of Man," Barth starts with a discussion on "The Man of Sin in the Light of the Obedience of the Son of God." One of Barth's tasks here is to assure that sin does not have an ontological life separate from the Word. If we conceive of sin as an independent reality, then we put it before God Himself. It is only through the real encounter with Jesus Christ that we understand sin itself. Jesus Christ reveals the destructiveness of sin, and the suffering it causes, but it is only in Jesus that we see the real pure form of this sin because he was the innocent one who

---

27. For an excellent treatment of abstract vs. concrete nature, see Crisp, *Divinity and Humanity*, chap 4.

28. I am aware of Barth's doctrine of sin elsewhere in which he describes sin not as something that has its own reality. See *CD* IV/1, 389–98.

29. See Allen Jorgenson, "Karl Barth's Christological Treatment of Sin," *SJT* 54, no. 4 (2001): 439–62. See also Adam J. Johnson, *God's Being in Reconciliation: The Theological Basis of the Unity and Diversity of the Atonement in the Theology of Karl Barth* (New York: T&T Clark, 2012), 147.

suffered without deserving it. In "The Pride of Man," Barth analyzes sin's construction. For him, the root of all sin is that man wants to be God. Key to Barth's formulation is the idea of concealment. Whereas Christ conceals his divinity in humanity in the act of humility, man tries to exalt himself to the point of divinity in the concealment of pride. The concealment of Christ humiliation is deeply shown at the cross. Here at the cross kingship and grace are shown to be the way forward for humanity who always chooses exaltation.

The other section is called "The Fall of Man." Here Barth tries to identify the man of sin. The man of sin falls exactly because he is the one who tries to exalt himself. God on the other hand has humiliation from the beginning. This humiliation is evidenced even by the fact that God has chosen to suffer: "It is God who suffers through the failure which comes with human pride."[30] This suffering is what makes it possible for us to experience forgiveness. Forgiveness is the restoration of order.[31] We are inverting the order on everything that God set as the determination for humankind and God. We are prideful and try to establish order through our ways, but these ways do not bring order, but disorder. Real order can only be introduced by the grace of God. This grace is shown in the economy *via* the atonement. One must not forget, however, that the atonement is the person of Jesus Christ.[32]

Jesus's solidarity then is not only an act of compassion, but God's own preoccupation with making all things converge to himself by virtue of his divine person (1 Cor 1:20).[33] Barth's main concern is not to propose a new ontology of humankind, sin, or God. Any careful reader would approach this section and note an intentional ethical and pastoral concern. For Barth, the "Word became flesh… means that the Son of God made His own the situation of man."[34] Even though the ontological implications may be obvious, the text should be read giving full credit to Barth's ethical intentions.

---

30. *CD* IV/1, 485.

31. *CD* IV/1, 491.

32. See also Shao Kai Tseng, *Karl Barth's Infralapsarian Theology: Origins and Development, 1920–1953* (Downers Grove, IL: IVP Academic, 2016), 245.

33. Adam Johnson writes, "Just as the doctrine of the divine perfections encourages us to explore Christ's work in light of each of the perfections of the Triune God, Barth's doctrine of sin encourages us to a variation of this task, approaching Christ's work in light of the various aspects sin revealed in Scripture and given their definitive exposition in light of the cross." Johnson, *God's Being in Reconciliation*, 148.

34. *CD* IV/1 216.

Christ's solidarity with humankind in sin precedes humankind's history. The gracious election of Christ in its supralapsarian character[35] allows Barth to insist that humankind does not *cause* solidarity in the Godhead. God, on the other hand, proactively embraces the plight of humans in Christ's assumption of a fallen flesh. For "God allows the world and humanity to take part in the history of the inner life of his Godhead, in the movement in which from and to all eternity he is Father, Son and Holy Spirit, and therefore one true God."[36] Solidarity has a twofold meaning: it is both the life of the Son into the far country with humankind and humankind taking part in the Godhead. The "strangely logical final continuation" of the economy is pertinent to the life of the Son in a "fallen and perishing state" *pro nobis*.

The key term, then, for our investigation is what Barth means by *Deus pro nobis* in this section in light of the fallen and perishing state and the twofold meaning of solidarity.[37] Barth answers the question by stating that "*Deus pro nobis* is something which he did not have to be or become, but which, according to this fact, He was and is and will be—the God who acts as our God."[38] *Deus pro nobis* functions as the turning of God toward humankind in which God is free and *pro se* by being humble and *pro nobis*. God's life *pro nobis* is demonstrated in His history "played out as world-history and therefore under the affliction and peril of all world-history."[39] That cannot mean the existence of any necessity that the *pro nobis* generates in God. If we speak of any necessity, we have to speak of the necessity of the

> fact that the being of God, the omnipotence of his free love, has this concrete determination and is effective and revealed in this determination and no other, that God will magnify and does in fact

---

35. van Driel, *Incarnation Anyway*, chap 5.

36. *CD* IV/1, 215.

37. Johnson summarizes the fourfold ways in which God is for us in §59.2: "(1) Christ took our place as Judge, he takes our place as the glorious one who shames us; where (2) he took our place as the judged, he is the one shamed; where (3) he was judged in our place, he was shamed in our place; and where (4) he acted justly in our place, he removes our shame and clothes us with his own glory (*CD* IV/1, 273; *CD* IV/2, 384)." Johnson, *God's Being in Reconciliation*.

38. *CD* IV/I, 214.

39. *CD* IV/1, 215.

magnify His own glory in this way and not in any other, and therefore to the inclusion of the redemption and salvation of the world.[40]

God is free when he shows his love and solidarity to another by being
humble. We are not allowed to think of the freedom of God only in terms of
the *Deus pro se*, without *Deus pro nobis* because this is who God determines
himself to be in his free love. God's free love is Barth's underlying framework which provides a rationale for a deep theological sense of how God
is in himself, *Deus pro nobis*. The love of God in revealing himself speaks of
the reality that he is—"God is love" (1 John 4:8). As noted, in this love that
he is, he determined to be *for us*. On the other hand, his freedom under-
scores the fact that in this determinative giving God remains himself.[41]
Colin Gunton explains this point lucidly:

> God's revelation as Father, Son and Holy Spirit is the event in which
> he creates fellowship with man, and it is in doing that he reveals
> that he is love. But this is a love that is given freely, for the mode
> of revelation makes it clear that, first, he is Father as well as Son,
> and, second, that he is Father, Son and Spirit independently of his
> relation to man.[42]

But how exactly can we still speak of freedom in humility and solidarity
if such solidarity could logically imply some sort of fall in humanity as it
"take[s] part in the history of the inner life of his Godhead"?[43] Barth does
not seem to answer this question here and moves quickly to his pastoral
and ethical concerns of how solidarity plays a role in the Son's life for us.
Maybe Barth is not interested in developing the logical consequences of
his formulations. For Barth, the Son of God did not "float over the human

---

40. *CD* IV/1, 213.

41. See Christopher R. J. Holmes, "The Perfections of God," in *The Westminster Handbook
to Karl Barth*, ed. Richard E Burnett (Louisville, KY: Westminster John Knox), 158. The issue
of God's free love is important here, but is embedded in a much deeper discussion that Barth
takes on *CD* II/1.

42. Colin E. Gunton, *Becoming and Being: The Doctrine of God in Charles Hartshorne and Karl
Barth* (London: SCM Press, 2001), 187–88. See also, Price, *Letters of the Divine Word*; Christopher
R. J. Holmes, *Revisiting the Doctrine of the Divine Attributes: In Dialogue with Karl Barth*, Eberhard
Jüngel and Wolf Krötke (New York: Peter Lang, 2007).

43. *CD* IV/1, 215.

situation like a being of completely different kind. He entered into it as a man with men."[44] This language and others such as "He was not immune from sin"[45] could be taken in several directions, especially if combined with the participatory language of the previous page.[46] But after this brief analysis, it looks like attributing fallenness to the divine life of the Son as an implication of Barth's participatory speech is not his goal in this section. His main goal in this section is to press upon the mind of his readers that God does not forget humankind in their sin. This deeply theological subject brings with it a deeper pastoral content. The plight of humankind is God's concern in his gracious way of being in the Son. This moves the reader to an ethical and pastoral consideration first and then, maybe, to ontology. But such conversation depends on concepts that are hardly Barth's concerns here.

As we will see, even though there is the eternal "taking on of human essence," divine immanent life is never given up. It is clear that Barth is interested in history and not in conceptualization. His main goal is to help his readers read the Bible at face value.[47] He conceptualizes as needed, but Barth mainly wants his readers to see that God is *for us* in every way possible and without reservation. Because the atonement cannot be separated from the person of Christ, the taking up of our sinful state works as a maneuver to keep this twofold person-work doctrine together in Barth's account of the atonement.[48] However, more than that, it serves a pastoral purpose. God is not free to be only *pro se*, but he freely determines himself to be God for us from eternity.

---

44. *CD* IV/1, 216.

45. CDIV/1, 216.

46. "God allows the world and humanity to take part in the history of the inner life of his Godhead, in the movement in which from and to all eternity he is Father, Son and Holy Spirit, and therefore one true God." *CD* IV/1, 215.

47. I owe this point to Tyler Wittman.

48. Christopher R. J. Holmes, "The Person and Work of Christ Revisited: In Conversation with Karl Barth," *Anglican Theological Review* 95, no. 1 (Winter 2013): 37–55.

SINLESSNESS IN *CHURCH DOGMATICS*

In *CD* IV/1, 258–259, Barth affirms the *non-assumptus* by asserting that "he took our flesh, the nature of man as he comes from the fall."[49] In Barth's interaction with the possibility of sin, however, he contends that sinlessness was not his condition, "It was the act of His being in which he defeated temptation in His condition which is ours, in the flesh."[50] The issue here goes beyond solidarity. According to Sonderegger, for Barth, Christ stands in need as he is the great penitent of the Bible.[51] If sinlessness was not the condition of Christ, one has to ask: is there an antecedent status that gives reason for the work of atonement? The rejection of Christ's impeccability is the starkest when the Swiss theologian pits concrete and abstract views of the obedience of the Son against one another. He says that the obedience of the Son is concrete in a way that he takes our place as sinners but does not sin. Whereas an abstract view of the sinlessness of Christ sees his obedience by virtue of his purity and goodness—he is sinless because he is the *Logos*.[52] According to Barth, we must reject an abstract view of the sinlessness of Christ because it does not pay careful attention to the testimony of Scriptures. Indeed, for Barth the correspondence language of 2 Corinthians 5:21—"For our sake he made him to be sin who knew no sin, so that in him we might become the righteousness of God"—plays a crucial role. The correspondence language is used here in order to further the solidarity of taking humanity's fallen nature, not forensically motivated, but from conception, Jesus bears the weight of the fall on his human nature.

One way this is demonstrated is in Christ's life of continuous repentance. In his "own person He reversed the fall,"[53] because he is the lost son who keeps coming back to the Father. Christ refuses "to take part in the game"[54] of un-repentance. Humankind's continual renewal of sin is exactly its unwillingness to repent.[55] Christ's sinlessness, however, is marked by

---

49. *CD* IV/1, 258.

50. *CD* IV/1, 259.

51. Katherine Sonderegger, "The Sinlessness of Christ," in *Theological Theology: Essays in Honour of John Webster* ed. R. David Nelson, Darren Sarisky, and Justin Stratis (New York: Bloomsbury T&T Clark, 2015), 267–75.

52. *CD* IV/1, 258.

53. *CD* IV/1, 259.

54. *CD* IV/1, 258.

55. *CD* IV/1, 258.

the very fact that he is never tired of repenting. In his human nature, Christ was exposed to temptation, but contrary to humanity's ways that are marked by impenitence, Christ is marked by obedience—coming back to the Father.

The issue here goes beyond the mere *assumptus*, but regards the person of the Son. Because sinlessness was not his own (personal) condition, the condition or possibility to sin had to be a condition that the person of the Son lived with. He had to understand the lowliness of creaturely sin and "acquire" sinlessness by obedience.[56] If, however, there is no personal antecedent guarantee of sinlessness, then what are we to make of the hypostatic union itself?[57]

Granted that Barth's attentive reading of Scripture with its economic framework is at full force, even the most charitable of readings, however, cannot but be perplexed by an affirmation that leads to a rejection of God's free antecedent life. For all the exegetical work one can make here, there seems to be no other way out, but the admission of an inconsistency with other sections in Barth's work where God's freedom and/or glory are admitted and celebrated.

We must return to the question in a different way: what can possibly guarantee the integrity of the personal union for Barth? Clearly for Barth, God is for us in Jesus Christ. That is his determination. Nothing causes the incarnation, but this event is the "strangely logical final continuation of the history in which He is God."[58] Therefore, a rupturing of the hypostatic union is not a viable option because it could mean the negation of God himself.[59] Even though he did not have to be *pro nobis*, this is who he

---

56. See *CD* IV/2, 92.

57. Sonderegger writes, "On pain of rupturing that union, I would say, the humanity born of Mary and the Spirit must be fully and wholly and perfectly reconciled to God. It is not simply compatibilism—or non-competitiveness, as it is often termed—that causes me to shy away from the mere possibility of fallibilism and sin. No, it is much stronger than that. Christ cannot sin because the bare possibility of it—*posse peccare*—is the possibility, *ex hypothesi*, of the human nature of Christ going its own way, seeking its own end, joining in the rebellion against God." Sonderegger, "The Sinlessness of Christ," in *Theological Theology: Essays in Honor of John Webster* (New York, Bloomsbury, 2015), 275.

58. *CD* IV/1, 203.

59. See Kornél Zathureczky, "Jesus' Impeccability: Beyond Ontological Sinlessness," *Science et Esprit* 60, no. 1 (January 2008): 55–71. "The meaning of the hypostatic union for Barth lies in God's election of Himself when in His Son He determines Himself to be fully human. Therefore, when God becomes human in the historical person of Jesus Christ the

determined himself to be as our God. God's determination is unbreakable. However, contrary to classical Reformed understandings, Barth does not secure the hypostatic union because of the personal existence of the Son— after all, Jesus Christ is not sinless. What secures the personal union is the grace of God by which Christ is sanctified.

Barth hints at this sanctifying project in his exegetical excursus in *CD* IV/1.[60] He sets the discussion of the temptation of Christ with a quotation from Hebrews 2:11: because "He that sanctifieth and they that are sanctified are one he is not ashamed to call them brethren." In his unity with human nature, the Son of God is both the one sanctifying and empowering, as also the one being sanctified to endure temptation through his human nature. Christ's role as representative is tied to him being able (δύναται) to identify as one with humanity.[61] Empowerment (δύναται) and sanctification being almost interchangeable means that Christ's sinlessness is not necessarily a reality of his unity with the divine person *per se*, but a reality of grace that empowers him to respond in a God-honoring way through temptation. If grace is the path that we follow, that is the path that He follows. Otherwise, he cannot be our representative. As with much of §59, the focus is on obedience and representation: "He persisted in obedience, in penitence, in fasting."[62] Obedience is the mark of a grace filled sanctified being. As Barth states, "He willed to live only by that which the Word creates, and therefore as one of the sinners who have no hope apart from God, as the Head and King of His people."[63] Once again, there is no antecedent guarantee for his sinlessness, but it is obedience through created communicated grace that makes it possible for his identification with us. One

---

limitations and humiliations of this existence are not in contradiction to God's immutability. On the contrary, the integrity of the divine essence would only be in jeopardy if the Son had not experienced humiliation. The election of God to become human in His Son is a determination of the divine essence." See also Jones, The *Humanity of Christ*, 129–30. The stress for Barth is always the unity of subject. "God does not merely indwell a human; Christ's unity entails the divine Son's being the defining and exclusive subject person."

60. But it is only at *CD* IV/2 that he fully develops his view. On Barth's appropriation of the *Communicatio Gratiarum* at *CD* IV/2, see Darren O Sumner, "Fallenness and Anhypostasis: A Way Forward in the Debate over Christ's Humanity," *SJT* 67, no. 2 (2014): 195–212. See also Barth, *CD* IV/1, 85–86.

61. *CD* IV/1, 259.

62. *CD* IV/1, 262.

63. *CD* IV/1, 262.

must not overlook the centrality of power. In the classical (or in Barth's language, abstract) account of the sinlessness of Christ, the power to resist sin comes from the acting agent—the person of the Son, who only acts as one who is always free. In Barth's "concrete" formulation there is power as well. The power, however, is the communicative sanctifying grace that creates, in Christ, obedience in temptation.

Christ's identification with sin is confirmed through Jesus's risk[64] that God and his angels are going to help him in the temptation account. Jesus must test and prove "of the final assuring of His relationship to God *in foro conscientiae*, in the solitariness of man with God."[65] Jesus does not hold to his privileges as the eternal Son of God, but as a man and in humankind's place, he risks the certainty of obedience for obedience that acquires certainty.[66] Risk is not necessarily a blind leap of faith, but one that "dare[s] to leap into the abyss, the way of the cross, when the will of God leads him to it ... but what led Him to it would have been His own will to make use of God's favour."[67] This risk is not a godless, uncontrolled event but is the world hanging on Jesus's trust of divine favor, his grace—strengthening for obedience.[68]

Grace is evidenced in Barth's exegesis of the Garden of Gethsemane. Whereas in Barth's exposition of the wilderness temptation, he asserts that Christ showed no hesitation; in the Gethsemane, Christ "had to face the reckoning."[69] "He knows that for Himself and His disciples, calling God is the only way to meet and defeat."[70] Although the disciples fail Jesus, in

---

64. *CD* IV/1, 263. "Jesus is to risk this headlong plunge with the certainty, and to confirm the certainty that God and His angels are with Him and will keep Him."

65. *CD* IV/1, 263.

66. See Kevin Hector, "Atonement," in *The Westminster Handbook to Karl Barth*, ed. Richard E Burnett (Louisville, KY: Westminster John Knox), 11–14.

67. *CD* IV/1, 263.

68. As Sumner said, "Thomas Aquinas spoke of this in terms of an infused *habitus* of grace: because 'Christ had grace and all the virtues most perfectly ... the 'fomes' of sin [i.e., concupiscence] was nowise in Him.' Protestant theologians recast this *habitus* by way of their expansion of the *communicatio naturarum*. This is where Barth locates the actuality of Christ's sinlessness: not in his lack of a fallen nature, but in that nature's divine giftedness." Sumner, "Fallenness and Anhypostasis," 207.

69. *CD* IV/1, 265.

70. *CD* IV/1, 267.

his prayer, Christ is strengthened to endure the final hour and to accept the cup of wrath.[71]

> He only prays. He does not demand. He does not advance any claims. He does not lay upon God any conditions. He does not reserve His future obedience. He does not abandon His status as a penitent. He does not cease to allow that God is in the right, even against Himself. He does not try to anticipate His justification by Him in any form, or to determine it Himself. He does not think of trying to be judge in His own cause and in God's cause. He prays only as a child to the Father, knowing that He can and should pray, that His need is known to the Father, is on the heart of the Father, but knowing also that the Father disposes what is possible and will therefore be, and that what He allows to be will be the only thing that is possible and right.[72]

In summary, for Barth, Christ does not have an antecedent certainty of sinlessness, nor does he trust in the future reiteration of his perfect obedience. He only trusts that he will be graciously empowered, strengthened, and sanctified.

COMMUNICATIO GRATIARUM AND
THE SINLESSNESS OF THE SON

Barth's theology of God's grace plays no small role. From election to the new Jerusalem, grace is a central concept for Barth.[73] The concern of this section, however, is not to debate how Barth avoids (or does not avoid) the necessity of grace in Godself. The discussion here will turn on how Barth uses grace in order to preserve the hypostatic union vis-à-vis his formulations of the fallen human nature and the sinlessness of Christ in our last sections.

---

71. CD IV/1, 268. "It is only after the strengthening which comes to Jesus that we hear of His αγονία."

72. CD IV/1, 270.

73. See a few examples in recent literature: Katherine Sonderegger, "Grace," in The Westminster Handbook to Karl Barth, ed. Richard E Burnett (Louisville, KY: Westminster John Knox, 2013), 87–89; Sumner, Karl Barth and the Incarnation, 131–32; Price, Letters of the Divine Word, 49–60; Jones, The Humanity of Christ, 136–46.

In Barth's "Homecoming of the Son of Man" at *CD* IV/2, there is an extensive discussion of the grace of God in relation to the incarnation. Here Barth contends that any sort of *Communicatio Gratiarum* to the human nature cannot be a "permanent state of blessing, but the continuity of which can be assured only... by the fact that He is always the same elect man confronted and surrounded and filled by the same electing grace of God."[74] Barth wants to avoid static conceptions of the grace of God in regards to the incarnation, because such conceptions would render the states of exaltation and humiliation less dynamic than they should be. For example, he asserts that the qualitative and quantitively differences between Him (Christ) and all other men is located in the exaltation of his human essence in which he *always* participates in the life of the Father, Son, and the Holy Ghost.[75] Even that difference, however, must not be seen in contradiction to the concept of humankind that embraces us: "It only contradicts all other actualizations of this concept."[76] Barth emphasizes that his christological anthropology is not an empty ideal that is not real to humankind. On the contrary, Jesus really fulfills what it means to be human. His human exaltation is not because he is of a different kind of human, but because he is the real human. However, one must ask what makes this exaltation possible and how can he fulfill his humanity perfectly?

The humanity of Christ is exalted and united to the life of Father and Spirit despite "creaturely, human and even sinful essence."[77] The "mechanism" that makes such union continuously possible at the reiterated life of the Trinity in the economy is the same electing grace of God. In this grace, sanctification is imparted to the human nature of Christ. Even though there is a presupposition of the antecedent life of the Son who positively affirms the sinless of Christ, Barth quickly qualifies it by stating that such a thing is a mere presupposition. The reality is that the electing grace, as it is repeated in the incarnation, is repeated with empowerment (ἐξουσία) in sanctification: "He receives power."[78] This power is given so that the work of reconciliation is accomplished not "in the nakedness of his divine

---

74. *CD* IV/2, 96.
75. *CD* IV/2, 94–95. Emphasis mine.
76. *CD* IV/2, 95.
77. *CD* IV/2, 96.
78. *CD* IV/2, 96.

power, in which they could not have been done as the reconciliation of the
world with God, but as the Son of Man, in His identity with the person
Jesus of Nazareth."[79] The mediator is not another *Logos* that is outside of
the person Jesus Christ. Here is a subtle polemicizing of the *extra-calvinisticum* in Barth's Christology. "In him, therefore, this one man, it is given
to human essence to attest the divine authority, to serve and execute it. ...
Thus divine authority has also the *form* of human authority."[80] The polem-
ics, however, of the *extra-calvinisticum* are quickly taken back by the assertion that human nature is an organ of "the Son of Man who is primarily
the Son of God."[81] The acting subject of the incarnation is the Son of God.
Human nature is the medium necessary for the work of atonement—an
organ.[82]

    Nonetheless, one must not press the theological point too far. Human
essence must not be conceived as "an appropriated state."[83] Contrary to
the reformed view of *habitus*,[84] in which the "essentialist/nature" concepts were overemphasized, Barth places the *locus* of the *communicatio
gratiarum* (empowerment) in Christ's history.[85] We circle back again to

---

79. *CD* IV/2, 97.

80. *CD* IV/2, 98. See Sumner, *Karl Barth and the Incarnation*, 171. As Darren Sumner posits,
"[t]here are no general concepts for giving definition to the content of Christology—only the
life of the savior narrated in Scripture."

81. *CD* IV/2, 98.

82. *CD* IV/2, 98. "It is empowered [human essence] as the necessary creaturely medium
for His action."

83. *CD* IV/2, 99.

84. See Richard A. Muller, *Dictionary of Latin and Greek Theological Terms: Drawn Principally
from Protestant Scholastic Theology* (Grand Rapids: Baker Book House, 1985), 134.

85. Sumner's full quote: "The Reformed held to a stronger account of the communication
of grace in order to secure some of the same benefits. 'These *gratiae habituales*, of which impeccability or *non posse peccare* is one (since Christ could not sin), were of course imparted to the
humanity of Christ without measure, since they are the highest gifts of the Spirit which a creature can receive at all'. The Reformed agreed that the gifts are finite and created, emphasising
that their context was Christ's state of humiliation. These gifts were given to him gradually
and not all at once, 'so as not to impair the natural development of his humanity.' The result
was that the *gratiarum* functioned as a conceptual container for everything that the Reformed
wanted to say about Christ's humanity *in distinction from* other men and women, but which
they did not wish to attribute to his divinity and the hypostatic union" (Sumner, "Fallenness
and *Anhypostasis*," 208). Although Sumner is correct—the role of the continual transmission
of gifts is true—these gifts were for the natural development of Christ. Barth's formulation
differs from the Reformers in that he uses the continual transmission of gifts to talk about
the sanctification of the fallen human nature and to maintain the sinlessness of Christ in
the economy. James Gordon explains the manner in which the Reformers understood this

Barth's actualism. Whereas reformed theology talked in terms of successive states of humiliation then exaltation, Barth stressed the "history in which He is God,"[86] or the fact that "His life is an event and not a state or *habitus.*"[87] The contours of this history are widely known, but are worthy to be recounted—in taking humanity, the one "who is primarily the Son of God"[88] humbles himself. On the other hand, the human essence is "exalted to dignity ... the glory and dignity and majesty of the divine nature."[89] This exaltation of the human essence, however, is not a deification. The exaltation is the elevation of human essence into the *"consortium divinitatis,* into an inward indestructible fellowship with his Godhead which He does not in any degree surrender or forfeit, but supremely maintains as He becomes man."[90] Here the immanent life of God is gloriously celebrated and protected. But once this qualification is made, Barth quickly moves back to how we identify this God. In a procedure similar to the previous sections, he states that from eternity the grace of God has come in the form of his election—being Emmanuel—God with us. The human essence that he takes on is "a clothing which He does not put off."[91] This clothing is not deified but sanctified for its exaltation, that is, the continuity of the hypostatic union.

SOME MUSINGS ON THE DOCTRINE OF ORIGINAL SIN AND REPRESENTATION

Anyone dealing with Barth's doctrine of original sin will notice that the placement is interesting. He intentionally worked the doctrine of original sin after treating Christology. So, it is only in §60 that he inserts his discussion, long after §58 and §59, the *locus classicus* for his mature Christology.

---

communicatio: "the *communicatio gratiarum* refers to the divine gifts of grace communicated to the human nature of Christ by the Word in the incarnation. These gifts include the gifts of the Holy Spirit as well as the grace of union which makes Christ's human nature worthy of honor." James R. Gordon, "The Holy One in Our Midst: A Dogmatic Defense of the *Extra Calvinisticum*" (PhD diss., Wheaton College, 2015), 100. The emphasis should fall on the grace of union. The empowerment in the habitual grace is not in the horizon of the Reformers.

86. *CD* IV/1, 203.
87. *CD* IV/2, 99.
88. *CD* IV/2, 100.
89. *CD* IV/2, 100.
90. *CD* IV/2, 100.
91. *CD* IV/2, 101.

As asserted above, Barth refuses to treat sin apart from Christ because doing so would give sin an ontological reality apart from Jesus Christ, and as it is well known, for Barth sin is an impossible possibility—literally, nothingness.

Through his actualism, Barth discusses the judgment revealed at the cross as a reiteration of who the Son is. This movement is contrary to humankind, which always reiterates its pride. Humankind is always prideful and cannot break from this vicious cycle. God in Christ is altogether flesh, but this flesh is the one that breaks from humankind's vicious cycle of pride.[92] The grace of God is always victorious and where pride/sin had the upper hand, "his grace did not cease or retire, but overflowed in the form of avenging righteousness, showing itself to be super-abounding, so that in the face of this opposition His forgiveness was His iron scepter."[93] This sin is not hereditary. Barth rejects a realist account of the transmission of sin and starts here an account of original sin itself.

Since one cannot see anything that does not converge in Christ, to construct an account of the doctrine of sin apart from Christ and focused only on Adam is to miss the point that Christ is greater than Adam. Christ is the *telos* and beginning of revelation. Adam also can only be seen through Christ. Adam "belongs to the past and has no future, but Christ is the one who reaches back and to the future."[94] Christ is one person who is always free and in his freedom incorporates the time necessary for the atonement and his revelation. Eternity is no longer an abstract concept but is the incorporation of time so that all the movements necessary for salvation are not in contradiction to the Godself, but in complete harmony.

This approach is crystalized in Barth's book *Christ and Adam: Man and Humanity in Romans 5*.[95] This book is an exercise in theological exegesis. Fully aware of how the passage of Romans 5:12–21 is usually interpreted, Barth sets his work in order to exalt Christ. Barth's initial discussion is set upon the speakability of God in Christ. Barth asserts that although Paul sees God and Christ as identical, he also distinguishes them in Christ's

---

92. *CD* IV/1, 496.

93. *CD* IV/1, 496.

94. *CD* IV/1, 502.

95. Karl Barth, *Christ and Adam: Man and Humanity in Romans 5* (Eugene, OR: Wipf & Stock, 2004).

human nature. This distinction, however, is not to say that Christ is a different kind of human than us.

In fact, Christ is the only true human. He is the one who tells us what it means to be man. Adam does not have the right to tell us what it means to be human. Christ does not adapt to Adam, but Christ, being the true image is the real human. One of the ways that Barth makes this point is by asserting that our existence in Adam does not have an independent status. He means that Christ is the only one able to stand as true representative for man. Christ is the only one able to vouch to the existence of Adam, but Adam cannot vouch for the existence of Christ. Adam is below and not above, "because his claim to be the 'first man' and the head of humanity like Christ is only apparent."[96]

This typological reading is engraved into Romans 5:12–21. Typology is verified by the "how much more" formula that Paul used here. Barth affirms that any time that this formula is used, the two things fall under the same organizing principle. "The lesser" in this organizing principle organized by Paul is Adam and not Christ. Christ himself, although stands in the high degree of this principle, he also identifies with humanity: "He is already king, secretly in His humiliation." This move of exaltation and humiliation is always present in Christ. And it is also because of this move that we can know Christ as king even in his crucifixion.

Our union with Adam is less essential than our union with Christ exactly because of the way in which God organized things. In Christ, the relationship between the one and the many is a gracious relationship. Between Adam and Christ stands Moses and the exposure of sin. With Christ, however, grace and life have a new way. The law came so that transgression is not covered, but grace came so that life and humankind might live as they were meant to be.

In the history of God with Israel, we can safely say that it is also the history of God with Adam. For both in the history of God with Israel and with Adam the response is the same.[97] Sin has had its ways. Barth asserts that "God's dealing with Israel make it impossible either to conceal or to explain

---

96. Barth, *Christ and Adam*, 22.
97. Barth, *Christ and Adam*, 48.

away the fact that man is sinful, hard as it is for us to admit that is true."[98] Because of the sinful character of Adam and Israel, they do not exemplify true humanity. True humanity is also victorious and free because it is in God who does not have fellowship with sin and conquers it in his humanity.

Although there was a substitution of the other nations taken by Israel, this substitution takes also the formula of "how much more." Jesus's substitution for Israel is the final great substitution. By taking the place of Israel he stands in place of all. Jesus is the true Israelite, the Messiah.[99] He is one who no Israelite father could beget, but one who is the Son of God.

According to Barth, by freely submitting "Himself to the Law He fulfilled it."[100] This is tying back to God's identity—as the one who exists determining his life for us—Barth constructs his reading of the Bible in an economical fashion. He refuses to reach back into the immanent life of God, but looks at Jesus and Adam, these two representatives and exalts Christ to his rightful place.

Nonetheless, what was humanity's response? It was not connected to any prevenient grace. Humans actually rejected God in his exalted and humble state. The coming of Jesus Christ is extremely opposed to humankind's plight, but it is also an indication of a one-directional decision to end humankind's opposition to God. Grace does not presuppose any cooperation, but it is God's way among and as humankind.

Because Jesus came as a human and as a Jew and was crucified, we have certainty that salvation is an event from God only. It does not depend upon some ethnicity, because the one who came as a Jew was crucified by the Jews. And even though he was crucified, God's grace was also manifested to them; making the point that God's grace is not for one people but to all men.[101] John Webster has made some interesting observations on this. He stated,

> The notion of original sin goes awry, however, when it is attached to that of hereditary sin. Barth's departure from the traditional terminology here (which he marks by preferring *Ursünde* to *Erbsünde*) is ultimately because an inheritance cannot be one's own act. "What

---

98. Ibid., 49.
99. Ibid., 61.
100. Ibid.
101. Barth, *Christ and Adam*, 69.

I do as one who receives an inheritance is something that I cannot
refuse to do, since I am not asked concerning my willingness to
accept it. ... It is my fate which I may acknowledge, but for which
I cannot acknowledge or regard myself responsible. And so, 'it is
not surprising that when an effort is made to take the word "heir"
seriously ... the term "sin" is necessarily dissolved.' Sin is delib-
erate action; linked to the notion of inheritance it comes to have
a 'hopelessly naturalistic, deterministic and even fatalistic ring.'
Properly speaking, then, by original sin is meant 'the voluntary and
responsible life of everyman ... which by virtue of the judicial sentence passed on it ... is the sin of every man, the corruption which
he brings on himself so that as the one who does so. ... He is necessarily and inevitably corrupt.' In this connection it is important
that Barth treats the scriptural account of Adam and the fall as *saga*
rather than history. To read it in such a way is to suggest that "it is
the name of Adam the transgressor which God gives to world-history as a whole," De-historicizing Adam, that is, lifts the concept of
Adam's sin out of the idiom of causality.[102]

Finally, Barth summarizes the entire argument of the book by simply
stating that even sinful humankind is essentially related to Jesus Christ—
that is the truth about Romans 5:12–21.[103] Such affirmation is only possible
because Jesus, even though an individual, is the representative of all men.
He is not only the representative of believers, but of all men because our
standing as believers (5:12–21) is only possible because of the *dia touto* that
is grounded in the global and wide aspect that is described in 5:1–11.

---

102. J. B. Webster, "The Firmest Grasp of the Real: Barth on Original Sin," *Toronto Journal
of Theology* 4, no. 1 (1988): 19–29.

103. Ibid., 74.

RECENT BARTHIAN APPROACHES

DARREN SUMNER

Sumner's project is an attempt to clarify Barth's proposal and also to mediate some of the misunderstanding regarding the *non-assumptus* and the classical position. According to Sumner, Christ is fallen only *anhypostatically*, but not in his *theandric* person.[104] For Sumner, this tracks closely to the classical person-nature distinction from Chalcedon, since natures cannot sin and therefore cannot be sinful. Nature, however, can receive or have the property of fallenness.

If fallenness is ascribed to Christ in the human nature only *anhypostatically*, then it can "achieve the sort of sympathy with and participation in real human existence that they desire."[105] For Sumner, the restriction of fallenness in *anhypostatic* manner allows one to say that the Son came into our state, but did not leave it that way. For Sumner, every side of the debate (of whether or not Christ had a fallen human nature) should adhere to *anhypostatic* fallenness. Sumner moves the debate further; he argues that even in the personal sanctification operated by the Son in his human nature, this human nature is still conditioned by the fall. What sanctification really achieves is to protect Christ from a state of peccability.

Furthermore, Sumner uses Barth's actualism to escape from the substantial/essential differences of states of pre-fall and post-fall human nature. In other words, contrary to the classical notion that persons possess natures and essences, Barth (and Sumner by extension) argue "that Jesus' humanity is not a static thing of which he came into possession but a lived history, and so talk of 'human nature' will necessarily be a somewhat artificial imposition."[106] In turn, this allows Sumner to argue for a *process* of sanctification of Christ's humanity, instead of an assumption of state. Since the humanity of Christ is in *lived history*, one must not appeal to a change in the nature of Adam from pre-fall to post fall. Hence, Jesus assumes humanity as Adam, even if that entails an assumption of a fallen nature.

---

104. See Darren O. Sumner, "Fallenness and Anhypostasis: A Way Forward in the Debate over Christ's Humanity," *SJT* 67, no. 2 (2014): 201.

105. Ibid., 202.

106. Ibid., 203.

PAUL DAFYDD JONES

Jones's monograph *The Humanity of Christ: Christology in Karl Barth's Church Dogmatics* registers some insights on how to read Karl Barth's Christology.[107] A key point for Jones is to begin the analysis *in media res*—starting from *CD* IV/2 and then moving to *CD* IV/1 (a move different than my own exposition). Jones's reasoning is that first, *CD* IV/2 discusses Barth's doctrine of reconciliation as it converses with Protestant scholasticism, and provides robust exegetical foundations. Second, *CD* IV/2 provides a robust exegetical foundation; in contrast to other parts of *CD*, here at *CD* IV/2 Barth keeps his promise of keeping the Bible at the center, instead of long philosophical *excurses*. According to Wolf Krötke, because self-actualization is only possible through the testimony of Scripture, the formation of true Christology has to be done in such fashion.[108] Third, any attempt to look into §59 (part of *CD* IV/1 and probably Barth's most conscious attempt to ground God's action in the atonement) in isolation from the entirety of the doctrine of reconciliation (*CD* IV/2, for example) runs the risk of avoiding the necessity of Christ as *our* human response. Treating *CD* IV/2 before *CD* IV/1 provides the necessary leverage to look at Barth's actualistic moments carefully.

As I have shown in my exposition of §59, an intentional actualistic reading of Barth here is not necessary to understand *what* he wants to theologize regarding Christ's human nature—at least in regard to the *non-assumptus*. Close attention to his own discussion of *Deus pro nobis* displays that it "is something which he did not have to be or become, but which, according to this fact, He was and is and will be—the God who acts as our God."[109] Actualism eventually works itself out, yes! specially in *CD* IV/2 through the *Communicatio Gratiarum*, but careful, intentional reading of *CD* IV/1 also provides the necessary guardrails for an acute analysis.

This discussion is not neglected by Jones, who argues similarly to my own exposition, that contrary to old Reformed understanding, Barth's common actualization provides a way to speak about the hypostatic union

---

107. Paul Dafydd Jones, *The Humanity of Christ: Christology in Karl Barth's Church Dogmatics* (New York: T&T Clark, 2008).

108. Wolf Krötke, "Die Christologie Karl Barths als Beispiel für den Vollzug seiner Exegese," in *Karl Barths Schriftauslegung*, ed. Michael Trowitzsch (Tübingen: Mohr Siebeck, 1996), 1–21. Referenced in Jones, *The Humanity of Christ*, 122.

109. *CD* IV/I, 214.

in a more dynamic way—instead of a *unio* it is a *uniting*. The theologou-
mena employed in this service are the *communicatio gratiarum* and the
communicatio operationum.

Via the *communicatio gratiarum*, Barth places himself in an interesting discussion. Contrary to Aquinas who sees the habitual grace of the
hypostatic union as the flow of the grace of union (because Christ is the
"pre-eminently graced human"[110]), Barth insists that the term be defined
as the "confrontation" of divine self-determination and human election:
God petitions (a) "Christ, as human, to enact a certain history and (b) how
Christ's human agency begins with the act of gratitude." With this move,
Jones argues that Barth was able to use the theologumenon of *communicatio
gratiarum* to tie together his doctrine of election, covenant, and incarnation.
God's grace must be conceived as inherently communicative. Hence, in the
"moment" of election God actualizes an infinite, never-ending communication of his grace to the human nature of Christ. Just as I showed in my
exposition, Jones re-asserts Barth's avoidance of the *habitus* notion raised
by Aquinas (such a conception is too static):[111]

> In the same moment that God's elective act brings into existence
> the human identifiable as Jesus of Nazareth, this human's "confron-
> tation" with grace carries the petition that he embrace and realize
> his identity as the Son of Man who is also the Son of God, and that
> he enact a history that leads from Bethlehem to Golgotha.[112]

What relevance has this discussion to the *non-assumptus*? Jones sums
it up by reflecting in this section of *Church Dogmatics*:

> [T]he sinlessness of Jesus was not a condition of His being as man,
> but the human act of His life working itself out in this way from
> its origin. And on this aspect, too, the determination of His human
> essence by the grace of God does not consist in the fact that there
> is added to Him the remarkable quality that He could not sin as a
> man, but in His effective determination from His origin for this
> act in which, participant in our sinful essence, He did not will to

110. Jones, *The Humanity of Christ*, 136.

111. Ibid., 139.

112. Jones, *The Humanity of Christ*, 139.

sin and did not sin. As a determination for this act it is, of course, His absolutely effective determination. [But] He accomplished it, He did not sin, because from this origin He lived as a man in this true human freedom—the freedom for obedience—not knowing or having any other freedom. The One who lived as a man in this harmony with the divine will, this service of the divine act, this correspondence with the divine grace, this thankfulness had no place for sinful action.[113]

While Christ is the sovereign free *Deus pro nobis*, who does not have to be or become and therefore is sinless, the common actualization of the natures must entail that his human nature has agency (a common property of human beings).[114] This free agency is exercised in "His effective determination from His origin for this act in which, participant in our sinful essence, He did not will to sin and did not sin."[115]

INITIAL EVALUATION

I have made it clear that Barth places the sinlessness of Christ neither in the acting subject (the person of the Son) nor in the unfallen human nature of Christ (since he does not have one). The *locus* of the sinlessness of Christ is twofold: history and the grace of God (by which Christ's humanity is empowered to obey and confirm his sinlessness). This grace, as seen, is not a *habitus*—a disposition of the soul or nature—as a singular act of union, but is grace that empowers him to respond in a God-honoring way through ministry, temptation, cross, and death.

The polarity is clear: Barth affirms the complete personal union, but the sinlessness of Christ can only be affirmed when the Son completes the obedience of his human life. One must ask, however, if anything "sanctifying" can maintain the hypostatic union and make it sinless?

The Catholic tradition of the church has, with reason, answered with a resounding but qualified "No." Taking my cues from Thomas Aquinas, I will show that Barth's rejection of the classical position on sinlessness puts

---

113. *CD* IV/2, 92–93

114. See Jones discussion of agency and human nature in Barth's theology in Jones, *The Humanity of Christ*, 169–75.

115. *CD* IV/2, 92.

the hypostatic union on an unstable foundation. Barth's emphasis on the necessity of grace for the acquisition of sinlessness is at a deeper level a debate on whether or not the personal union is complete from the moment that the person of the Son assumes body and soul, or when his obedience is finalized through his death on the cross.

As stated in the introduction of this book, Aquinas correctly assumes that human nature stands in "need of the gratuitous will of God, in order to be lifted up to God."[116] However, the elevation of human nature up to God is of two forms: (1) by operation or (2) by personal being. Aquinas's point is that both the sanctification of humankind and assumption of human nature by Christ are gracious events. Nonetheless, the mode of elevation by operation is a habitual activity that is accidental. Contrary to the grace that unites human nature to the divine person, the accidental character of grace by operation results in a work that renders *participation in likeness*. The elevation by personal being, on the other hand, is greater because it is not accidental. The human nature is once and for all united to the personal being of the Son, not in a participation in likeness, but in a substantial union. Whereas, according to Aquinas, all saints have participation in the operative grace, only Christ's human nature is *united* to the divine nature by grace of the personal being.

Aquinas also contends that "no merits of His [Christ's] could have preceded the union."[117] Such affirmation would hardly be rejected by Barth. If we trace, however, the logic of Barth's argument thus far in this study, some issues may come to the surface:

1. *The personal union is a fact;*

2. *The Son, in solidarity, assumes a fallen human nature;*

3. *In assuming this nature, he sanctifies it;*

4. *This work of sanctification (through the* communicatio gratiarum*) is what gives continuity to the hypostatic union so that Christ may acquire sinlessness.*

---

116. *ST III* Q2. A10. co.
117. *ST III* Q2. A11. co.

The sanctification of human nature for the continuity of the hypostatic union—in Barth's scheme—is a property that human nature receives; therefore, it is accidental and not essential.

In Barth's contention that Christ's "life is an event and not a state or *habitus*,"[118] he has an operative notion that the history of Jesus Christ is the meaning of the personal union and not the other way around. Here lies both the genius and the error of Barth. He does not theologize with concepts, but he conceptualizes as he theologizes. Christ's history vitally tells us who God is—*Deus pro nobis* without reservation.[119] This history of the divine and human together, however, is kept together with God's history *via* the communication of graces in the same manner we experience it.

As mentioned in the start of this paper, this is where the Nestorian problem enters. Underscoring any Nestorian formulation is the idea that the union of divine and human natures is not ontological, but they cooperate in conjunction, never in union. Thomas White asserts that two distinct problems can actually undergird different versions of Nestorianism: (1) when someone posits a real distinction of persons in Christ; (2) when someone "attempts to conceive of a personal union of God and humankind in Christ, but does so through the medium of spiritual operations of Christ alone (Christ's consciousness of God)."[120] Our focus here is on the second distinction, for in this formulation "Jesus is one with God/the Logos insofar as he is remarkably conscious of God."[121] If the four premises above are true of Barth's formulation of both the fallenness and the sinlessness of Christ, then one can hardly miss the underlying Nestorian category of conjunction under the second distinction provided by White. The "obedience that acquires sinlessness" with the communication of graces as the instrument for continual preservation of the hypostatic union indicates that the agent that acquires sinlessness may not be identical with the *Logos*. After all, the *Logos* is sinless.

---

118. *CD* IV/2, 99.

119. Ivor Davidson captures the heart of Barth's economical reading and the genius of his conceptualization as he theologizes, see Davidson, "Pondering the Sinlessness of Jesus Christ," 393.

120. White, *The Incarnate Lord*, 111.

121. Ibid., 112.

The classical Thomistic formulation states, as surveyed, that the hypostatic union is maintained through the grace of assumption itself. Because the divine person of the Son assumes a human nature, this nature is endowed with a special grace that only comes when united to the person of the Son. This empowerment, however, is not given to the human nature so that it can respond to something. This is where Barth's formulation seems to lend a hand to Nestorianism: the empowerment for the acquisition of sinlessness in obedience is dangerously close to attributing some actions to the human Jesus that are not the same of the *Logos* himself.

A final word of caution is needed. Given Barth's uneasiness with the vocabulary of Chalcedon and his preference for dynamic language, it is possible and likely that his rejection of *habitus* is not particularly a rejection of the Thomistic account of "grace of union." The more plausible explanation is that he is actualizing the human nature of Christ. Although sympathy is needed for Barth's project—dynamism does capture several of the biblical movements—the innovation may be costly. The sinlessness of Christ is not conditioned to the continual receiving of grace. As Aquinas shows, the union of the Son with the created human nature communicates grace. This grace, however, is not an empowerment for the ministry of life and death of Christ.

Barth's accounts of the assumption of the fallen human nature of Christ, his sinlessness, and the communication of graces are beautifully interwoven in several maneuvers that keep his dynamic reading of the Bible alive. The God who is for us without reservation is in solidarity so that "sinlessness was not therefore His condition."[122] To keep him from sin, the grace of God is communicated to Jesus in his ministry of life and death.

If sinlessness is not the condition of Christ, then the agent of the incarnation could be interpreted as a different agent than the Logos, who is sinless. When, in Barth's account, Christ must test "the final assuring of His relationship to God *in foro conscientiae,* in the solitariness of man with God"[123] one cannot help but ask, who is the agent of the solitariness with God?

In conclusion, Barth's rationale for the *non-assumptus* goes through complete solidarity and the empowerment of Jesus. Against some recent

---

122. *CD* IV/1, 259.
123. *CD* IV/1, 263.

Barthian scholarship, I do not think that it is necessary to posit a heavy accent on actualism, or to propose that actualism inserts sin in the divine life because of solidarity. However, due to a lack of antecedent personal guarantee, then the Son of God becomes one who depends on the Spirit to conquer sin.

3
—

T. F. TORRANCE AND THE
MEDIATION OF SALVATION

THE LATIN HERESY AND INCARNATION

For Torrance (1913–2007), salvation does not occur externally to Christ, but it "takes place within him, within the incarnate constitution of his person as Mediator."[1] This intuition constitutes the grounds for Torrance's rejection of the Latin theory: an idea that "Jesus's work is separate from or external to his person."[2] The hypostatic or personal union of the divine and human natures in the Son of God guarantees that whatever happens, happens through the mediation of Christ himself—therefore a personal salvation. Furthermore, this mediation is personal because the person of the Son heals the state of the human nature (fallen), which he assumes from within his own being. Hence, all the actions of this mediator are not external to us, in forensic fashion, but are intrinsic to us—to our own nature that he unites to his own person.

It is important to note here that Torrance is moved by robust, Trinitarian and christological theologies. *Homoousios* plays a central role for his formulation of the atonement and his rejection of the Latin commercial/external transaction. For him, it was not possible to separate the person and work of Christ. He said,

> There is one Mediator between God and men, the man Christ Jesus, who gave himself a ransom for all. For Athanasius this meant that the mediation of Christ involved a twofold movement, from God to

---

1. Thomas F. Torrance, *The Trinitarian Faith* (New York: T&T Clark, 1993), 155.

2. Kevin Vanhoozer, "Atonement" in *Mapping Modern Theology: A Thematic and Historical Introduction*, ed. Kelly M. Kapic and Bruce L McCormack (Grand Rapids: Baker Academic, 2012), 183.

man and from man to God, and that both divine and human activity in Christ must be regarded as issuing from one Person. Here we see again the soteriological significance of the Nicene homoousion: If Jesus Christ the incarnate Son is not true God from true God, then we are not saved, for it is only God who can save; but if Jesus Christ is not truly man, then salvation does not touch our human existence and condition. The message of the Gospel, however, is that Jesus Christ embodies in his human actuality the personal presence and activity of God. In him God has really become man, become what we are, and so lives and acts, God though he is, "as man for us" (ὡς ἄνθρωπος ὑπὲρ ἡμῶν). *Only God can save*, but he saves precisely as man—Jesus Christ is God's act. God acting personally and immediately as man in and through him, and thus at once in a divine and in a human manner (θεϊκῶς and ἀνθρωπίνως). With this basic Nicene principle in mind, we shall consider first the significance of the incarnation and the incarnate Mediator, and then the import of the atoning mediation, reconciliation and redemption accomplished by Christ on our behalf and for our sakes.[3]

The basic thrust of what Torrance said here should be affirmed by any theologian. Yes, it is wrong to separate the person and work of Christ. Such separation is often made only for dogmatic and didactic purposes. Torrance, however, is going farther with the principle of *homoousios*. The fact that Christ is *homoousios* with the Father and *homoousios* with humankind tells one that the work of atonement is a passive action because it is the work of God on humankind, but Jesus is also God. Again, this should also be affirmed by any coherent doctrine of atonement. The problem lies when the *locus* of the passive action of God is seen as synonymous with the incarnation itself. One major movement informs Torrance's identification of the incarnation as the *locus* of atonement: the doctrine of theosis. This idea will open the way for Torrance to reject the "transactional" or "external" aspects of penal substitutionary atonement. This movement is finally encapsulated in Torrance's theology of mediation.

---

3. Torrance, *The Trinitarian Faith*, 149.

THEOSIS

Given Jesus's share of human nature and his personal representation, Torrance builds his case for how humanity benefits from the work of Jesus.

In an article called "Incarnation and Atonement: Theosis and Henosis in the Light of Modern Scientific Rejection of Dualism,"[4] Torrance sets the stage for his discussion of theosis by asserting that "The hypostatic union carries with it the realization that the atoning exchange whereby we are reconciled to God takes place within the incarnate constitution of the Lord Jesus Christ."[5] He continues affirming that "it [sic, "if"] the incarnation is not thought in terms of saving and healing assumption of our fallen human nature and is therefore not internally integrated with the atonement, then the doctrine of the atonement can be formulated only in terms of external transaction."[6]

Finally, he built upon a few main points that show the ontological reality of the atonement in conversation with scientific and theological dualisms. His goal was to show how Christianity is a religion of unity (henosis) and not a dualistic perception of the world. In what follows, I will summarize Torrance's concerns with theosis and then address his mechanism for incorporation.[7]

---

4. Thomas F. Torrance, "Theosis and Henosis in the Light of Modern Scientific Rejection of Dualism," *Society of Ordained Scientists* 7 (Spring 1992): 8–20.

5. Ibid.

6. Torrance, "Theosis and Henosis in the Light of Modern Scientific Rejection of Dualism," 12.

7. Torrance appears to move from an initial rejection of theosis to a semi-Palamite view of energies and participation. Matthew Baker notes that "In the first letter of Torrance [to George Florovsky], written in Jan. 1950, Torrance registers his rejection of the doctrine of theosis as 'un-Hebraic and un-biblical.' By 1964, however, he would address the World Alliance of Reformed Churches with a plea 'for a reconsideration by the Reformed Church of what the Greek Fathers called theosis.' In his 1970 lecture 'The Relevance of Orthodoxy,' Torrance described theosis as the experience of "our participation in the Holy Spirit, in which we come under the direct impact of God's uncreated energies in all their holiness and majesty, and are sanctified and renewed by them. ... God Himself acting upon us personally and creatively.' It was surely no coincidence that in this same published sermon, when remarking on how ecumenical dialogue with the Orthodox had often led him to reconsider his Reformed presuppositions in his reading of the Bible, Torrance stressed the crucial influence of Florovsky in particular. He would later cite Florovsky's essay on 'St Gregory Palamas and the Tradition of the Fathers' approvingly for its understanding of theosis in terms of 'personal encounter.'" See Matthew Baker, "The Correspondence between T. F. Torrance and George Florovsky (1950–1973)," *Participatio: Journal of the Thomas F. Torrance Theological Fellowship* 4, no. 1 (2013): 287–323.

First, the introduction of Newtonian science and the incorporation of Kantian metaphysics created a massive dualism between absolute time-space and relative time-space. The Christian tradition, according to Torrance, fundamentally needs to reject scientific dualism and retrieve the truths of theosis and henosis from the early church. For in those truths the atonement was an internal act of God in the incarnate Jesus in space and time and not an outside "impossibility" (as described in Kantian metaphysics).

Second, God is activity in his being. To assert activity in the being of God was Athanasius's contention when he coined the term *enousios logos* "to speak of the inherence of the word of God in his being."[8] According to Torrance, it is only with John of Damascus and Thomas Aquinas that such understanding is abandoned in favor of a dualist mentality that sought to protect God's impassibility and immutability. Karl Barth saved the day by not choosing between God's being or his act. Karl Barth saw that the early church, specially Athanasius, was interested in the activity of God and that the tradition from which the Reformation had sprung had a special interest in the being of God. God is fundamentally a being-in-act. Therefore, the work of atonement is not an act that goes forth, externally, as a decision from the being of God. Jesus Christ is the atonement because he does what he is—in time and eternity.

Third,[9] through Christ and in the Spirit, we can know the internal relations of God's triune being. Torrance contends that a doctrine "of atonement is to be formulated in terms of what took place in the inner constitution of the mediator."[10] Torrance builds this theory by expanding on the intelligibility of the doctrine of creation. The Christian doctrine of creation ex nihilo sustained that the contingent nature of the universe was held open to scientific investigation. With this move, the doctrine of creation avoided the dichotomy between the empirical and the theoretical. It is with Kant, however, again, that the "laws of nature were regarded not as read out of nature but as read into nature, for realities, he held cannot

---

8. Torrance, "Theosis and Henosis," 13

9. Ibid. Torrance had two other points, but for the sake of space and relevance, I will stay with the most important points.

10. Ibid.

be known in their internal relations but only as they appear to us."[11] For Torrance, Kant's epistemological revolution has to be dismissed. Science itself has proved to operate "through penetrating as deeply as possible into the rational structure embedded in empirical reality."[12] Even though there are differences between knowledge of creaturely realities and God's uncreated reality, Torrance insists that the foundation of knowledge helps us in a reappropriation of the doctrine of the Holy Trinity not only for our worship, but for the certainty that all our knowledge of God's ways and works (including incarnation and atonement) is grounded in the fact that God is Father, Son, and Spirit.

Finally, for Torrance, to separate the work and person of Christ is to operate in dualistic categories. The activity of the Lord in time is what he is. Hence, he was able, with Barth to say that Jesus Christ is the atonement. The Son's life toward the outside cannot add anything to himself. There is no separation of person and work—Jesus Christ, in his inner constitution is the atonement, but one ought to be careful not to say that we become God. Torrance is aware that one cannot speak in this way. "Rightly understood, then, theosis actually expresses the sheer 'Godness' of God the Holy Spirit."[13] Theosis is participation in the divine life in which "we receive the grace and light of his Spirit, [and] are said to be theoi."[14] Therefore, there is a gracious enabling that puts one as participating in the very light of God but not transformed into God.

In summary, Torrance is trying to displace the subjective aspect of salvation. For him salvation and atonement happen at the birth of Jesus Christ where he takes our nature heals it in uniting himself to it. James Cassidy states that for Torrance, "our humanity (and in fact, humanity as such) is born and born again in the birth and rebirth of Jesus Christ."[15]

---

11. Ibid.

12. Ibid.

13. Molnar, "Thomas F. Torrance," 198.

14. Torrance, The Trinitarian Faith, 139.

15. James J. Cassidy, "T. F. Torrance's Realistic Soteriological Objectivism and the Elimination of Dualisms: Union with Christ in Current Perspective," Mid-America Journal of Theology 19 (2008): 165–94.

THEOSIS AS UNION: TORRANCE'S MECHANISM AND
A BRIEF EXCURSUS ON REFORMED THEOSIS

Myk Habets claims that Torrance is developing what is already present in Calvin's thought. Habets sets the stage by quoting Calvin at length in a section that Calvin defines the *unio mystica*: "we do not, therefore, contemplate him outside of ourselves ... in order that his righteousness may be imputed to us ... but because he designs to make us one with him."[16] Yes, there is continuity between Calvin and Torrance. Calvin was not formulating his doctrine of atonement from a purely forensic (i.e., the Latin heresy) perspective, but his doctrine of union was embedded in his covenantal paradigm. Torrance's "innovation," however, comes when building upon Calvin's mystical union he proposes that our union with Christ is also in "prothesis—divine purpose, mystērion—mystery, and koinonia—fellowship/communion."[17]

Prothesis refers to the election whereby Jesus is both the object and the subject of election. This is the classical Barthian formulation where there is no *decretum absolutum*.[18] For Barth (and subsequently for Torrance) there is no decree regarding the choosing of individuals. Jesus Christ is the decree and his incarnation is the eternal decision (being-in-act) of God in his Love. *Mysterion* points to the mystery of the hypostatic union. Because the hypostatic union is the union between two estranged realities coming together, this is also a reconciling union in which we are reconciled and elevated. Christ not only comes in humankind, but as humankind and therefore, the two realities are not only seemingly conjoined, but forever united in one person. Also, this reconciling union is not even remotely juridical, but actual. Thus Torrance can posit:

> [I]t is not atonement that constitutes the goal and end of that integrated movement of reconciliation but union with God in and through Jesus Christ in whom our human nature is not only saved, healed and renewed but lifted up to participate in the very light, life

---

16. Calvin, *Institutes* 3.11.10.

17. Habets, *Theosis in the Theology of Thomas Torrance*, 105.

18. For an excellent treatment on the difference between Barth's and Calvin's views of the absolute decree see David Gibson, *Reading the Decree: Exegesis, Election and Christology in Calvin and Barth*, T&T Clark Studies in Systematic Theology (New York: T&T Clark, 2009).

and love of the Holy Trinity. … In the Church of Christ all who are redeemed through the atoning union embodied in him are made to share in his resurrection and are incorporated into Christ by the power of his Holy Spirit as living members of his Body. … Thus it may be said that the "'objective" union which we have with Christ through his incarnational assumption of our humanity into himself is "subjectively" actualized in us through his indwelling Spirit, "we in Christ" and "Christ in us" thus complementing and interpenetrating each other.[19]

Habets also shows how Torrance applies the concept of *mysterion* to the tension of the one-and-the-many—Christ and his church. For Habets, in defense of Torrance, the key is to see the ontological union between Christ and his body, the church. Torrance saw the union with Christ largely as a corporate reality in which individual members are engrafted into Christ by baptism.[20] Finally, *koinonia* has a double reference; one is vertical and the other is horizontal. "Vertical" refers to our participation "through the Spirit in the mystery of Christ's union with us."[21] "Horizontal" refers to our communion with one another in the body of Christ. Even with all this apparatus, Torrance thinks that he is also able to dodge deification and not blur the creator-creature distinction. The work of the reader is to measure such affirmations and to see if it is merely formal/rhetorical, instead of material affirmation.

After this survey of Torrance's innovations, one must ask if they are at least plausible. First, in prothesis, there is substantial literature on Barth's view of election. The strongest argument against prothesis, however, seems to be that if God elects to be human *pro nobis*, but not *in se*, then there is contingency in the Godhead. Even Barth and Torrance themselves would deny such affirmation. The literature here is endless, but in my estimation, the amount of qualifications needed by the Barthian side renders the position at least unstable.[22]

---

19. Thomas F. Torrance, *The Mediation of Christ* (Exeter: Paternoster, 1983), 66–67.

20. Habets, *Theosis in the Theology of Thomas Torrance*, 106.

21. Ibid., 107.

22. That is not to say that the classical Protestant position does not need qualifications. For a quick survey of problems with the Barthian position, see Bruce L. McCormack, "Let's

The most problematic is the *mysterion* of Torrance. Here it seems that Torrance's formal denial of human deification crumbles. How can humanity be "not only saved, healed and renewed but lifted up to participate in the very light, life and love of the Holy Trinity."[23] without a natural change? Also, humankind cannot be *in toto* engrafted into the hypostatic union. Yes, the personal union is mysterious; it is, however, a union of a concrete nature and not a general abstract human nature. Finally, as I will point out in my main critique, if our reconciliation is being accomplished by the personal union in Christ, when this "reconciliation" happens does the hypostatic union finally happen? At which stage are we engrafted into Christ's hypostatic union?

Recent discussion about incarnational community needs to take care not to confuse how person and natures relate. Natures are substances that can belong as properties of persons that are in subsistent relations and that are in themselves the acting subjects through that specific nature. So, when Paul calls the church the "One new man" in Ephesians 2, even though there is some sort of participation in the divine, this participation does not imply a perichoresis,[24] because perichoresis presumes a shared nature. The church is "an incarnation" of the love of God; and this incarnation is not a self-existing person with subsistent relations. The incarnational community is in itself *creatura verbi* through and through.

On this theme, Webster indicts "communion ecclesiology"[25] with being unclear because it asserts that "[it] is heavily invested in a theology of the ontological union between Christ and the body of the Church."[26] It even

---

Speak Plainly: A Response to Paul Molnar," *Theology Today* 67, no. 1 (April 1, 2010): 57–65; Kevin W. Hector, "God's Triunity and Self-Determination: A Conversation with Karl Barth, Bruce McCormack and Paul Molnar," *IJST* 7, no. 3 (July 1, 2005): 246–61; Gibson, *Reading the Decree*; Edwin Chr. van Driel, "Karl Barth on the Eternal Existence of Jesus Christ," *SJT* 60, no. 1 (February 2007): 45–61.

23. Torrance, *The Mediation of Christ*, 66.

24. See Oliver D. Crisp, *Divinity and Humanity: The Incarnation Reconsidered*, 1st ed. (Cambridge, UK ; New York: Cambridge University Press, 2007), 31. Crisp is careful not to subscribe to a stronger version of *perichoresis* that assumes that all properties are shared, because it would eventually lead to an identity crisis.

25. See Henri de Lubac, *Catholicism : A Study of Dogma in Relation to Corporate Destiny of Mankind* (Burns & Oates, 1958), 145. See also Robert W. Jenson, *Systematic Theology, Vol. 2: The Works of God* (Oxford University Press, 2001), 213.

26. John Webster, "The Church and the Perfection of God" in *The Community of the Word: Toward an Evangelical Ecclesiology*, ed. Mark Husbands and Daniel J. Treier (Downers Grove,

affirms that it is impossible to know "at which point Jesus stops and the Church begins."[27] The reason some like Torrance build this system is to avoid a mere external Christology to ecclesiology. And here we need to remember again that externalism is Torrance's greatest fear. For example, both De Lubac and Jenson reject what they called "the metaphysics of Mediterranean antiquity" by arguing that the Eucharist's representation of the cross is not so much a figure of divine speech but "enduring communion between Creator and creature."[28] This communion is qualified by affirming that there is no transition from natural to supernatural love.

Webster answers this charge by appealing to a metaphysics that is not divorced from Scripture, but that springs from Scripture's covenantal categories. Webster said, "theologies of creation and reconciliation alike require us to conceive of the relation of God and creatures as relation—in distinction, that is to say, as covenant fellowship."[29] The relation in distinction that Webster builds in this article is the same as that which I have been building throughout this work: "God and God relative to all things." He explains, by saying that the incarnation is a "wholly unique, utterly nonreversible divine act; in it the Son of God unites himself to the man Jesus."[30] It is an act of God's freedom that does not pertain to other creatures. Therefore, the humanity of Jesus is not a "creaturely quantity that is annexed by God."[31] And because it is an irreversible, unilateral act of God, it is not extensible to general humanity—or the community of the saved ones. Hence the reason for calling the union of the Logos with the created human nature a hypostatic—or personal—union. Christ enhypostasised a particular human nature. This once again shows that the tools that Chalcedon provided in its aftermath are still useful in the midst of much confusion.

A moderate Reformed version of theosis may be of help here, without actually creating an ontological continuity between Christ and the church

---

Il, IVP Academic, 2013), 85.

27. Ibid.
28. Ibid., 87.
29. Webster, "The Church and the Perfection of God," 87. Emphasis in the original
30. Ibid., 93.
31. Ibid.

and at the same time not operating only in forensic categories.[32] J. Todd Billings states,

> In terms of contemporary theological discussion, perhaps the greatest danger in claiming that Calvin teaches "deification" is that his view could be too quickly assimilated into late Byzantine notions of θέωσις, from which he retains distance ... frequently Palamite theology is used as the "standard" by which to judge other theologies of deification. As a result, theologies of deification in the West end up looking like more or less truncated versions of a late Byzantine theology with which they never explicitly engaged. Scholarship on Calvin is no exception to this trend.[33]

Billings ends up arguing for a distinctive perception of theosis that tends to be more careful through the eyes of Calvin. Even though Calvin uses the word θέωσις, he meant to point to redemption in which the original union of God and humankind would be restored. This restoration is in "Christ through the Spirit as the believer grows to be 'conformable' to God; this process is culminated in the participation in Christ's resurrection and glorification, and in a beatific vision."[34] At this point at least there is a contrast with Torrance who seemed to imply that our participation in Christ's hypostatic union is even before the cross in the inner constitution of the savior.

Most importantly however is that for Calvin, the participation of humankind in the life of God is not synergistic. Calvin's anthropology would not "permit" him to affirm that humankind had anything to do with the inner life of God. It is however, in the life-giving (economy) of the God-church that one participates in that theosis for Calvin. Torrance would never subscribe to a synergistic soteriology, but it is hard to see how, if one is grafted into the hypostatic union through the human nature of Christ, one is also not accomplishing things in cooperation with Christ.

---

32. See Kyle Strobel, "Jonathan Edwards's Reformed Doctrine of Theosis," *Harvard Theological Review* 109, no. 3 (July 2016): 371–99.

33. J. Todd Billings, "United to God through Christ: Assessing Calvin on the Question of Deification," *Harvard Theological Review* 98, no. 3 (July 2005): 315–34.

34. Ibid.

THE MEDIATION OF CHRIST

Torrance scholars still debate if there was a mature Christology developed after the Auburn lectures in 1939. In order to escape charges of limiting our examination of Torrance to early theology, I will deal here with his *The Mediation of Christ* (first published in 1992).[35] This is not only his more mature work, but it is a summary of his christological musings.

He begins by stating that God is one with humankind is true, but does that imply we are not to distinguish between the *Logos asarkos* and the *Logos ensarkos*? Since "God was in Christ making reconciliation," how do we explain that without seeming like we are operating with flagrant Nestorianism?

The answer goes back to how we know things. Torrance understands the world of physics to be an illuminating analogy. In the beginning of the last century, with Ernst Mach's claims that atoms are merely "scientific fiction" and Kant's position that we do not know things as they really are but just as we project them, positivism and observational scientific theory had the upper hand. The work of Max Planck on quantum theory put an end to mere observation. Atoms were proved to be real not by observation, but by the "discovery that energy has an *atomic* structure governed by the universal constant h."[36] All this shows that science had to give up its obsession with appearances and observation and develop a simpler, yet sophisticated theory of knowledge where "knowledge of things is controlled through the disclosure of things in their internal relations and structures."[37]

By analogy, in theology, the inner relations of Father-Son are revealed in the incarnate person of Jesus Christ. This goes directly against both phenomenological approaches since Schleiermacher and also against the speculative approach in the Middle Ages. That is why Torrance reaches to the fathers as he thinks that they neither do Christology from below or above. Patristic theology, starting with the Person of Christ as revealed in the gospels, avoids dualistic approaches that divide the Savior into categories.

---

35. Torrance, *The Mediation of Christ*.
36. Ibid., 51.
37. Ibid.

Such knowledge is foundational for understanding that the Son does not "mediate a revelation or a reconciliation that is other than what he is."[38] In this unity one must posit the idea that there is no God behind the back of Jesus Christ. To see any line of demarcation is only to go back to Arianism.[39]

Mediating salvation in this form, Jesus came into "our human being and united our human nature to his own, then atoning reconciliation takes place within the personal Being of the mediator."[40] What Jesus Christ does is not separate or external from who he is because it discloses truthfully his inner relations. Therefore, when he *really* takes "our sin and guilt, our violence and wickedness ... he might do away with our evil and heal and sanctify our human nature from within."[41] Because Jesus reveals perfect harmony of his filial relationship, then men and women who are *taken up* also share in this relationship and are healed from their sins in the one who reconciles in himself.

How then can we think about a union with our humanity that does not completely divinize it? The explanation lies in Torrance's concept of *Personalizing person*: against dualism he claims that Christ's uncreated person personalizes our created persons. Because we are persons but are not sincere and hypocrites, we tend to live dual personal lives. The Word personalizes us by taking out insincerity and living a true human life that avoids its dualistic senses.[42] To further the argument beyond moralistic understandings of the incarnation, Torrance creates a dual scheme of analysis of how Jesus makes us truly one: (1) atoning union and (2) hypostatic union. He subsists in our nature and takes away what "cuts us off from genuine relations with others, so that the very personal relations in which persons subsist as persons [are atoned for]."[43]

---

38. Torrance, *The Mediation of Christ*, 56.
39. Ibid., 61.
40. Ibid., 63.
41. Ibid.
42. Ibid., 69.
43. Torrance, *The Mediation of Christ*, 69.

RECENT TORRANCIAN APPROACHES

KATHRYN TANNER

Tanner follows a similar line as that of T. F. Torrance.[44] Her books, *Christ the Key*[45] and *Jesus, Humanity and the Trinity*[46] attempt to bring back a theology of participation that takes seriously the importance of Christ to every theological *loci*, especially to anthropology. The incarnation takes humanity up into the life of God and in that movement, Christ becomes the very means of how we also become what we were meant to be.

Tanner, like Torrance (perhaps even more radically), argues that the incarnation is the atonement. The cross is not the means of salvation, but the effect of salvation. Seeing the cross as central to the forgiveness of sins works with a commercial and external view of the atonement. The mechanism for atonement, as incarnation, then is found in the communication of properties in the incarnation. In the incarnation the "characteristics of human life become the (alien) properties of the Word, and thereby the properties of the Word ... become the (alien) properties of humanity in a way that saves humanity from sin and death."[47] Therefore, the atonement ceases to be interpreted as a transaction between the Father and the Son and becomes the Son's vicarious substitution for humanity.

Tanner furthers her argument by stating that the notion of sacrifice as propitiation has been kidnapped and modified in the hands of fundamentalists. For Tanner, propitiation is related to "the cultic sacrifices of Israel [which they] celebrate or end in joyous communion."[48] The idea of sacrifice must not be connected to appeasing an angry God, because sacrifice by definition, "involves the reinstatement or restoration of communion with God *via* divine prevenient action. ... Applied to the atonement, this means that the sacrifice of the cross, as a part of the larger divine act of redemption that is the Incarnation, is 'a rite performed by God and not human beings.' "[49]

---

44. See Crisp, Revisioning Christology, 111–31.
45. Kathryn Tanner, *Christ the Key* (Cambridge: Cambridge University Press, 2010).
46. Kathryn Tanner, *Jesus Humanity and the Trinity* (Minneapolis: Fortress Press, 2001).
47. Tanner, *Christ the Key*, 254.
48. Tanner, *Christ the Key*, 266.
49. Crisp, *Revisioning Christology*, 118.

JOHN CLARK AND MARCUS PETER JOHNSON

Clark and Johnson's approach is yet another recovery of Torrance's formulation. Therefore, the fear of an extrinsic atonement (i.e., the Latin heresy) and the *an-en-hypostatic* distinctions are widely used in their recent monograph.[50] They state that because the incarnation is not an external transaction, Christ did not interrupt the normalcy of human organic structure and stream of human heredity, but he invaded them. By invading human organic structure and stream of heredity, the Son penetrates the depths of our human fallenness and concretely heals it.[51]

Clark and Johnson try to bring clarity to the issue with five points under a section called, "What Are We Saying and Not Saying?"[52] First, their affirmation of the assumption of the fallen nature grounds the cross in the incarnation. The cross would have no meaning if it was an alien imposition. If seen as culmination, instead of an interruption, the cross works from the beginning as God's plan. Second, they want to emphasize that the incarnation should not be viewed in an instrumental fashion. The Son did not assume a body and a soul only to atone for sins at the cross. For Clark and Johnson, the Son assumed a human nature so that the incarnation was at once atonement and the atonement was at once incarnational. Third, the human nature of Christ was corrupted and tended toward sin, but keeping with Chalcedon and the Bible, Clark and Johnson deny that he ever sinned.[53] Fourth, "the immediate sanctification of the sinful flesh that God the Son assumed in the womb of Mary must not be understood

---

50. John Clark and Marcus Peter Johnson, *The Incarnation of God: The Mystery of the Gospel as the Foundation of Evangelical Theology* (Wheaton, IL: Crossway, 2015).

51. Ibid., 113.

52. Ibid., 119.

53. Clark and Johnson support this point with a quote from John Webster: "This re-making [of our humanity] takes place as he assumes sinful flesh, human existence in repudiation of and rebellion against its ordering by God to find fulfillment in fellowship with God. The Word assumes the full extent of human alienation, taking the place of humanity, existing under the divine condemnation. But his relation to the human alienation which he assumes is not such that he is swallowed up by it. He does not identify with humanity under the curse of sin in such a way that he is himself sinner. ... He adopts the condemned human situation without reserve, but with a peculiar distance from our own performance of our humanness. By not following our path, by refusing complicity with the monstrousness of sin, he is and does what we are not and do not: he is human. In his very estrangement from us as the bearer rather than the perpetrator of sin, he takes our place and heals our corruption. That the Word became flesh means that he takes to himself the accursed situation of humanity in sin. But he takes it to himself; he does not evacuate himself into our situation." John Webster,

as Christ's immediate glorification."[54] Admitting immediate glorification in this case would lead toward a denial of the state of humiliation. Such a thing is denied both by proponents of the *non-assumptus* and the traditional view. Fifth, the *non-assumptus* position keeps the unity of God and humankind closer than the traditional view without actually attributing sin to Christ. In this way God redeems us because the acts of the Son took place within the inner constitution of the mediator and not outside.

INITIAL EVALUATION

Before any initial evaluation, it may be profitable to posit what Torrance is and what he is not affirming. Contrary to Irving, who taught that the Son remained sinless only through the work of the Spirit when he took a human nature,[55] Torrance maintained that the sinlessness of Christ is due to his divine person.[56] So, the person-nature distinction is still operative in Torrance's formulation of the *non-assumptus*.

What Torrance is saying is that "the Word became flesh," means that he "took 'our human nature as we have it in the fallen world.' "[57] Integral to this scheme is Torrance's use of Nazianzen's axiom: "the unassumed is unredeemed." Not only would it be unredeemed, but it would show a lack of love from God. Chiarot writes and quotes Torrance here:

> Rejection of the *non-assumptus* leads to "the Latin heresy," which
> consists of construing salvation in wholly forensic and external cat-
> egories, and results in an instrumental conception of the human-
> ity of Christ. Torrance states the implication of the denial starkly.
> "How could it be said that Christ really took our place, took our cause
> upon himself in order to redeem us? What could we then have to do

---

"Incarnation," in *The Blackwell Companion to Modern Theology.*, ed. Gareth Jones (Malden, MA: Wiley-Blackwell, 2007), 220, quoted in Clark and Johnson, *The Incarnation of God*, 123.

54. Clark and Johnson, *The Incarnation of God*, 123.

55. Kevin Chiarot, "The Non-Assumptus and the Virgin Birth in T. F. Torrance," *Scottish Bulletin of Evangelical Theology* 29, no. 2 (2011): 229–44.

56. Thomas F. Torrance, *The Doctrine of Jesus Christ: The Auburn Lectures 1938/39* (Eugene, OR: Wipf & Stock, 2001), 122–24.

57. Torrance and Walker, *Incarnation*, 62, quoted in Chiarot, "The Non-Assumptus and the Virgin Birth in T. F. Torrance."

with him?" It would mean that the love of God had stopped short of union with us in our actual condition.[58]

Two issues of contention arise: the question of the love of God and the question of instrumentalism. On the former issue, no side of the debate has the upper hand. While advocates of the fallenness position may argue for identification and union, advocates of unfallenness position can argue that because God loves us, he does not identify with sin.

The issue of instrumentality, however, is serious. The charge here is that Christ's center of consciousness is the Word and the human nature of Christ is merely an avatar through which the Word works. To speak thusly is rhetorically appealing; however, it became factorially more complicated to go against an instrumentalist perception of the incarnation with Constantinople III and the Dyothelite consensus. The two minds of the Son in his full humanity should inform Torrance that fallenness is not the only way to construct the Son's full identification with human nature. The early church was able to affirm the full humanity of Jesus by simply asserting that he needed a body and soul (with Constantinople III developing that in the issue of minds) and not necessarily with a fallen nature.[59]

However serious the issue of the charge of instrumentality is, it is not at all wrong to speak in instrumental terms, provided one is careful with the ideas. In Thomas White's superb study in Thomistic Christology, he asserts that the humanity that is assumed "cannot be a subsistent human person on its own," but only insofar as it is assumed by the one person of the Son.[60] White's concerns regarding the nature of the incarnation and what is the nature of the assumption are relevant for our next analyses.

---

58. Chiarot, "The Non-Assumptus and the Virgin Birth in T. F. Torrance."

59. Aloys Grillmeier, *Christ in Christian Tradition: From the Apostolic Age to Chalcedon*, Rev ed. (Louisville, KY: Westminster John Knox Press, 1988).

60. White, *The Incarnate Lord*, 13.

THE VIRGIN BIRTH

There is a clear tension in Torrance's thought here, for even though "the union of God and man in Jesus Christ is not thought of somehow ontologically complete at Bethlehem,"[61] Christ, "breaks through the continuity of Adamic existence"[62] in the incarnation.

The reason for this break with Adamic existence, for Torrance, is the virgin birth. In his exposition of the doctrine, he affirms a fairly traditional position in which the continuity is within the flesh Christ receives from Mary. The discontinuity is the vertical intersection of the Holy Spirit who interrupts the process and creates a discontinuity. The puzzle for the careful reader is how to affirm a discontinuity if the flesh Christ assumes is a fallen one?

Torrance's way out of that conundrum was to say that "when the holy Son of God unites himself to our corruption, the incarnation in the 'narrow sense' cannot but be a healing event."[63] The complexity of Torrance's thought here also poses a problem for the critique, since for him incarnation and atonement are fully united. There are indeed moments of the life of Christ, however, when one must not separate person and work of Christ. Therefore, Torrance can speak of the sanctification of the virgin birth as a completed event even if Christ assumes a fallen human flesh. The perception of time (incarnation-then-atonement) in Christ's life of atonement is merely a dualistic perspective to which Torrance is allergic.

I shall point to a few problematic constructions here. First, it is doubtful that a creative way out is to affirm a "narrow sense" of healing in the incarnation. The incarnation is an event brought forth by the work of the Holy Spirit who through the virgin birth, once for all, unites the Son to *a* human nature.

Second, the sanctifying event is not of degree but kind. Torrance, however, sees that virgin birth is an indication of what happened within humanity in general (degree) when he Son of God became human.[64] The

---

61. Torrance, *Scottish Theology*, 14.

62. Torrance and Walker, *Incarnation*, 94.

63. Kevin Chiarot, *The Unassumed Is the Unhealed*, 99.

64. Torrance and Walker, *Incarnation*, 94–95.

virgin birth serves as a signpost for *theosis* which creates a mere difference of degree between humankind and God since there is a full participation.

Finally, clearly for Torrance, something redemptive happens at the virgin birth but, as Chiarot aptly showed, the key question to be posed is, how? If human nature is healed, then Christ assumes a human nature that is not fallen (not the case for T. F. Torrance). If regenerated, Christ assumes a *posse non peccare* nature, but this is not exactly what Torrance affirmed. If the human nature that Christ assumed was one with enabled will to resist sin, then the nature that Jesus received was almost like the one we have, but not entirely. For Torrance, any hint of "almost" would lead to an external atonement. It is unclear in the end of the day what the virgin birth really creates in terms of discontinuity for Torrance.

4

INSEPARABLE OPERATIONS

THEOLOGICAL DEVELOPMENT

The doctrine of inseparable operations boasts an impressive and catholic pedigree. John Owen, for example, explicitly appeals to Athanasius, Basil the Great and Ambrose of Milan to further his argument in ΠΝΕΥΜΑΤΟΛΟΓΙΑ.[1] Today, however, the doctrine has come under sharp attack and needs to be properly defined. My goal here is to demonstrate how the classical articulation of the doctrine of inseparable operations prohibits one from asserting that the Son assumes a fallen human nature.

In order to do that, I will spend time describing the development of the doctrine from the first articulations of Gregory of Nyssa, and Augustine of Hippo until the refinement of language brought about by Thomas Aquinas and John Owen in their scholastic approach. These figures are chosen so that we can both see the ecumenism and coherence in the church. From east to west and from prosaic style to scholastic approach, the church needs to affirm oneness in God. Second, I will specifically relate the doctrine of inseparable operations to the doctrine of the incarnation. Finally, I will demonstrate how a robust doctrine of inseparable operations as described in points one and two prevents one from subscribing to the Son's assumption of a fallen human nature and relate it to the fallen human nature issue.

The principle of *opera ad extra sunt indivisa* states that the external works of the persons of the Trinity are one.[2] They initiate in one and terminate in another person, following the *taxis* of God's inner modes of

---

1. *Works*, 4:93.

2. For a discussion of the Reformed Orthodox's reception of the doctrine of inseparable operations, see PRRD III, 257–63. For a dogmatic approach to this doctrine see John Webster, *God Without Measure : Working Papers in Christian Theology, Volume 1: God and the Works of God* (New York: Bloomsbury, T&T Clark, 2015), 162–64.

being. How the church gets to this assertion is important, for there is a development and refinement of the language used here.

AUGUSTINE (354–430)

Augustine's discussion of the doctrine of inseparable operations is an interesting case study. Lewis Ayres has pointed to a slight development in his defense of the doctrine. Early in *Letter II*, there is an affirmation that is basically a repetition of what Hilary and Ambrose had said without much connection to the incarnation (written in AD 389, only three years after his conversion). Here the bulk of the discussion sits within the common nature shared by the Father and the Son. There is, however, later development in AD 410 when Augustine writes *Sermon 52*. Here, Augustine's Trinitarian theology has reached a more mature articulation.[3] Hence, let us follow the structures of *Sermon 52* (together with other sections from *De Trinitate*) to see how Augustine properly discusses the doctrine of inseparable operations.

Augustine starts *Sermon 52* by describing the nature of the catholic faith: it is not loosely connected articles of faith that are declared by several people's opinions, but it is "the firmest and most orthodox faith, that Father, Son, and Holy Spirit are one inseparable trinity or triad; one God not three gods."[4] Nonetheless, as he turns to a discussion of Matt 3:16–17 Augustine raises the question: "where is the inseparability of the trinity?"[5] Since we have the voice of the Father, the Spirit coming as a dove, and the Son being baptized, it all seems to be separate activities that contradict the united voice of the catholic faith.

The meditation that begins to answer this question is found in another deeper question: does the Father do anything without the Son? Augustine answers with the biblical axiom that nothing that was created was created without the Son.[6] As we look now to the Father, should we also say that the Father was born of the virgin Mary or that the Father suffered on the cross? Augustine answers with a decisive no. Let us examine the birth of

---

3. See Lewis Ayres, *Nicaea and Its Legacy : An Approach to Fourth-Century Trinitarian Theology* (Oxford: Oxford University Press, 2004), 374.

4. Augustine, *Sermons 51–94*, trans. Edmund Hill (Brooklyn, NY: New City Press, 1992).

5. Augustine, *Sermon 52.3*.

6. Augustine, *Sermon 52.4*.

the Son from the virgin Mary. By confession we are obliged to say that it is only the Son who was born from her, but Augustine states that the birth of the Son is a "work of both Father and Son. It was not indeed the Father but the Son, who suffered; yet the suffering of the Son was the work of both Father and Son."[7] So Augustine spends time from sections 52.9 forward making the exegetical case that the birth of the Son was brought about from the Father (Gal 4:4–5) and from the Son also (Phil 2:6–7).[8] He summarizes the exegetical section saying:

> I have made good what I promised; I have established my propositions with, as I think, the strongest proofs and testimonies. Hold fast then what you have heard. I will recapitulate it briefly, and entrust it to be stored up in your minds as a thing, to my thinking, of the greatest usefulness. The Father was not born of the Virgin; yet this birth of the Son from the Virgin was the work both of the Father and the Son. The Father suffered not on the Cross; yet the Passion of the Son was the work both of the Father and the Son. The Father rose not again from the dead; yet the resurrection of the Son was the work both of the Father and the Son. You see then a distinction of Persons, and an inseparableness of operation. Let us not say therefore that the Father does any thing without the Son, or the Son any thing without the Father. But perhaps you have a difficulty as to the miracles which Jesus did, lest perhaps He did some which the Father did not! Where then is that saying, The Father who dwells in Me, He does the works? All that I have now said was plain; it needed to be barely mentioned; there was no necessity for much labour to make it understood, but only that care should be taken, that it might be brought to your remembrance.[9]

And once he felt comfortable with the exegetical case made for the inseparability of the operations of Father and Son, Augustine moves to a metaphysical defense of it. The first step is by stating that the Godhead

---

7. Augustine, *Sermon* 52.8.

8. Augustine also references the biblical case for the inseparability of God's work in the passion of the Son, with the Father giving us the Son (Rom 8:32) and the Son giving himself up for us (Gal 2:20). See Augustine, *Sermon* 52.8.

9. *Sermon* 52.14.

is beyond material location. This key affirmation for the doctrine of simplicity serves as the backbone for inseparable operations: because God is one and immaterial, his will or nature cannot be divisible, even if we are talking about three persons. Thereunto, Augustine remains silent and cannot seem to say much more (here the concept of subsistent relations as will be developed by St. Thomas will bear more fruit.)[10] The only way forward for Augustine seems to be through his triads of psychological analogies.

In *De Trinitate*, Augustine continues the reflection on the external operations of the Trinity. This time, however, Augustine recourses to the internal order of the Trinity as the basis of external action. In other words, the internal *taxis* of the persons of the Trinity is reflected in the order of action toward us. The reason that the Son cannot do anything *from* himself (John 5:19) is because the Son is not of himself, but *eternally from* the Father.[11] Eternal generation grounds the temporal activity of God. As Keith Johnson suggests, reflecting in Augustine's Trinitarian theology:

> The Father acts with the other divine persons according to his mode of being "from no one" (unbegotten). The Son acts with the other divine persons according to his mode of being "from the Father" (generation). The Spirit acts with the other divine persons according to his mode of being "from the Father and the Son" (procession). Combining these two elements we might say that the divine persons act inseparably through the intra-Trinitarian *taxis*: from the Father, through the Son, and in the Holy Spirit. We can see this dynamic clearly in Augustine's discussion of the work of the

---

10. Oliver D. Crisp and Fred Sanders, eds., *Advancing Trinitarian Theology: Explorations in Constructive Dogmatics* (Grand Rapids: Zondervan, 2014), 68.

11. *De Trinitate* 2.3. Augustine states, "The working of both the Father and the Son is indivisible and equal, but it is from the Father to the Son. Therefore the Son cannot do anything of Himself, except what He sees the Father do. From this rule, then, whereby the Scriptures so speak as to mean, not to set forth one as less than another, but only to show which is of which, some have drawn this meaning, as if the Son were said to be less. And some among ourselves who are more unlearned and least instructed in these things, endeavoring to take these texts according to the form of a servant, and so misinterpreting them, are troubled. And to prevent this, the rule in question is to be observed whereby the Son is not less, but it is simply intimated that He is of the Father, in which words not His inequality but His birth is declared." See also Keith E. Johnson, *Rethinking the Trinity and Religious Pluralism: An Augustinian Assessment* (Downers Grove, IL: IVP Academic, 2011), 119; Lewis Ayres, *Augustine and the Trinity* (Cambridge: Cambridge University Press, 2014), 247.

divine persons in creation. Genesis 1 teaches that God created light. What light did the Son create? It certainly cannot be a different light. Rather, it must be the same light: "Therefore, we understand that the light was made by God the Father, but through the Son" (Tract. 20.7, 170). Similarly, the Father created the earth. The Son did not create another world by "watching" the Father. On the contrary, the world was created by the Father through the Son. Summarizing his discussion of the creative work of the triune God, Augustine explains, "The Father [made] the world, the Son [made] the world, the Holy Spirit [made] the world. If [there are] three gods, [there are] three worlds; if [there is] one God, Father and Son and Holy Spirit, one world was made by the Father through the Son in the Holy Spirit." (Tract. 20.9, 172)[12]

GREGORY OF NYSSA (335–394)

In Gregory of Nyssa's *Ad Ablabius* he is preoccupied that because we experience God through the ends of an operation, we might assert that there are different operations from the persons. So, Gregory starts with establishing that any act is done in accordance with the nature of the agent. In God's case, Nyssa asserts that the biblical testimony points to an unnamed nature. Whatever can be said of the divine nature can never be known *in toto*. The Cappadocian gives the example of incorruptibility: although we know that God is incorruptible, "our conception of incorruptibility is this,— that that which is, is not resolved into decay: so, when we say that He is incorruptible, we declare what His nature does not suffer, but we do not express what that is which does not suffer corruption."[13] Nonetheless, when speaking of natures, Nyssa raises the question with an imaginary debater: all humans have the same nature, yet we still speak of multiple humans in the plural? Two men making a shoe are not one man, even if it is the same activity. Why should we apply a different principle to the Godhead?[14]

---

12. Keith E. Johnson, "What Would Augustine Say to Evangelicals Who Reject Eternal Generation?" *SBJT* 16, no. 2 (Summer 2012): 34.

13. Gregory of Nyssa, "On 'Not Three Gods,'" in *A Select Library of the Nicene and Post-Nicene Fathers of the Christian Church*, 28 vols. in two series, ed. Philip Schaff et al. (Buffalo, NY: Christian Literature, 1887–1894), series 2, 5:333.

14. It is important to note that Nyssa applies the term "Godhead" exclusively to God's operation, and not to refer to God in his nature (as this avoids naming the divine nature).

Since the actions of every person, even if they are in the same pursuits, are separated from each other, we have to speak of multiple persons. In God, the reverse is true because

> in the case of the Divine nature we do not similarly learn that the Father does anything by Himself in which the Son does not work conjointly, or again that the Son has any special operation apart from the Holy Spirit; but every operation which extends from God to the Creation, and is named according to our variable conceptions of it, has its origin from the Father, and proceeds through the Son, and is perfected in the Holy Spirit. For this reason the name derived from the operation is not divided with regard to the number of those who fulfill it, because the action of each concerning anything is not separate and peculiar, but whatever comes to pass, in reference either to the acts of His providence for us, or to the government and constitution of the universe, comes to pass by the action of the Three, yet what does come to pass is not three things.[15]

Our sensibilities should then be reworked with the biblical testimony. We do not experience the acts of God in a separate fashion, but we experience the actions of God always through the one operation of the three persons. Nyssa is careful here not to assert that three acting amounts to three things—contrary to the actions of individual human beings involved in similar pursuits.

The supreme example of reworked sensibilities on God's action toward us is that the gift of life given to us is not tripled because we "see" three persons in that bestowing. Life is given to us by the Father, prepared by the Son, and depends on the will of the Holy Spirit. This, however, does not amount us being given three lives.

Moreover, the operations of God follow a certain pattern of causality. They are communicated by the Father through the Son to the Holy Spirit. Even though we have three persons involved in a cause of an action, these are not three separate causes. Nyssa explains that the act is only complete, so to speak, when it has sprung from the Father, operated by the Son, and perfected in grace by the Holy Spirit. Only then can an action be said to have

---

15. Gregory of Nyssa, "Ad Ablabius," 334.

been caused by God.[16] This follows the fitting pattern of action: whatever happens inside is mirrored outside. The Holy Spirit is the gift of new life to us, because he is the eternal Gift of the relationship of Father and Son.[17]

Similarly to Augustine, Gregory builds on the issue of causality and the inner life of God. Although we are pressed to say that it is only one cause in the economy of salvation, Gregory establishes that the one cause must be seen through different angles: One is the *cause* and another is *of* the cause. He clarifies stating that this talk about distinction of cause is not referring to the nature of God, but to the manner of existence. "To say that anything exists without generation sets forth the mode of its existence, but what exists is not indicated by this phrase."[18] Here we see again the caution of not naming the divine nature. The relations of origins, however, are enough for us to see and apply within an economical shape a unique and one operation of God that differs in manner of cause (because of the different relations) but is one because it is one undivided nature.

INSEPARABLE OPERATIONS AND THE INCARNATION: SOME NECESSARY SCHOLASTIC DISTINCTIONS

Although Augustine and Nyssa's description of the inseparable operations of the Trinity are laudable, there are still some points that need clarification. Thomas Aquinas's concepts of real and subsistent relations illuminate the fittingness of the incarnation in a way that the Spirit's work has a certain quality coherent with who he is in Godself. This move will help to discern whether there is a sanctification that the Son works in the human nature, and if so, what is the quality of this sanctification?

---

16. I will come back to acts and causality later. This definition by Nyssa is a good start, but it still raises some questions. Nyssa never really clarifies how the persons relate to one another in order to complete the action. Furthermore, there are aspects of acts that need to be addressed. Ultimately, these are questions raised by later analytical approaches. These cannot be ignored in order to bring precision to our discussion.

17. On the naming of the Holy Spirit as Gift and Love see Augustine, *De Trinitate*, chapter 15. For an excellent exposition of this section see, Matthew Levering, *Engaging the Doctrine of the Holy Spirit: Love and Gift in the Trinity and the Church* (Grand Rapids: Baker 2016), 106.

18. Gregory of Nyssa, "*Ad Ablabius*," 334.

REAL RELATIONS

The concept of real relations as expounded by St. Thomas aims to establish a certain difference between creator and creature and also differentiate the persons of the Trinity. According to Gilles Emery, real relations have a two-sided perspective: "(1) it is a pure relating to another, and (2) it has existence within a subject."[19] In (1) each person of the Trinity is distinguished and constituted through the relation he has with the other person. Creatures are not brought into this region. In (2) the relation is the same as the divine essence, meaning that each person fully possesses the divine essence. Here Aquinas permits a talk about creatures. For him, God creates through the divine essence, meaning that "God creates because he is *God and in so far as he is God.*"[20] The personal relations in its pure forms are totally constitutive of each person, but the person is involved in the external relation to the world in the manner in which he is God. Put another way, "the eternal processions are the cause and the rationale of the making of creatures."[21] Here is what has been hailed as one of the greatest moves from Aquinas—his theology of fittingness. Aquinas asserts that a thing is fitting "which belongs to it by reason of its very nature."[22] And although it is the very same nature that is of the Father, Son and Holy Spirit, the manner or reason in which this nature subsists in the Son makes him the suitable one to assume human flesh.[23]

The idea of a fitting operation then is not grounded merely in the aesthetics of the personal relation, but more fundamentally, on the actuality of that pure act in the inner life of God. The incarnation is fitting, not because it adds something to the pure relations of God, but because the

---

19. Gilles Emery, *The Trinitarian Theology of St Thomas Aquinas* (Oxford: Oxford University Press, 2010), 340.

20. Emery, *The Trinitarian Theology of St Thomas Aquinas*, 341.

21. I Sent d. 14, q. 1, a. 1.

22. *ST* 3.1.1.A

23. The usual caveat is needed here to maintain a classical, proper Christology. Aquinas himself provides it: "Although in God Nature and Person are not really distinct, yet they have distinct meanings ... inasmuch as person signifies after the manner of something subsisting. And because human nature is united to the Word, so that the Word subsists in it, and not so that His Nature receives therefrom any addition or change, it follows that the union of human nature to the Word of God took place in the person, and not in the nature." See Frederick Christian Bauerschmidt and Thomas Aquinas, *Holy Teaching: Introducing the Summa Theologiae of St. Thomas Aquinas* (Grand Rapids: Brazos Press, 2005), 180, see also 180–81n15.

incarnation is an external operation that accords with God in the manner of existence as Son who is generated by the Father.

DIVINE MISSIONS AND ACTS

So far, the theology of a real relation has helped us see the fittingness of an action. This action, in time, is what has been called a mission. A mission as Legge describes it, reflecting on Thomas, has two key elements: "(1) the person's eternal procession, and (2) the divine person's relation to the creature in whom this person is made present in a new way, according to some created effect."[24] In (1), also reflecting in the constitutive relations of origin, Aquinas argues that there are two acts in the divine nature: one of intellect and another of will. The act of intellect is seen as God the Father who understands himself and eternally generates the Word. Since nothing can be loved by will unless it is conceived by the intellect, then the Spirit of Love proceeds from the Father and the Son.

The activity of the Trinity outside of the blessed life in its mission includes "the eternal procession [described above], and adds something, namely, a temporal effect."[25] And even though as Nyssa stated, there is only one cause of divine action, because there is only one God, this one God acts in a manner fitting to his relative properties. The addition of the created effect is not to the general deity per se, but to one specific person. Hence the incarnation is the temporal effect of the divine mission added to the Son.

Catherine LaCugna has objected to the notion of inseparable operations exactly on the basis that one cannot identify a specific act of a person if all acts are in themselves of all three persons of the Trinity. She states,

> Once it is assumed that the Trinity is present in every instance where Scripture refers to God, and once the axiom *opera ad extra* is in place, no longer, it seems, is there any need for the plurality of persons in the economy. At least it is no longer possible to single out any one person in relation to a particular activity.[26]

24. Dominic Legge, *The Trinitarian Christology of St Thomas Aquinas* (Oxford: Oxford University Press), 15.

25. *ST* I. 43., A. 2 ad 3. This section on divine missions has been largely inspired by Adonis Vidu, "Trinitarian Inseparable Operations and the Incarnation," *Journal of Analytic Theology* 4, no. 1 (2016): 112–15.

26. Catherine Mowry LaCugna, *God for Us: The Trinity and Christian Life* (New York: Harper San Francisco, 1993), 97–98.

As has been shown here, however, the actuality of the processions allows for a mode of action toward outside that befits one specific person even though all three persons are in one sense involved in this *act*. According to LaCugna, God's self-communication "is not a copy or analogy of the inner Trinity but is the Trinity itself; this means that the communication can occur only in the intra-divine manner of the self-giving of Father to Son and Spirit. Both *ad intra* and *ad extra*, then, the divine persons 'do not differ from their own way of communicating themselves.' "[27] Any mediation between true expression of Godself and history that express difference in the threeness of God is not a true self-communication of God.

Adonis Vidu has also made the case for a specific definition of act that avoids LaCugna's fears. Reflecting on Thomas and applying some analytical principles, Vidu concludes that an act is an event "which has both active and passive components. There is an active agency involved here, in so far as an agent is causing the assumption of the human nature. There is a patient too, though, insofar as the assumption is predicated of a particular person."[28] Vidu urges the reader to think about a butler dressing his master. The master is really the one taking the clothes, but the act of dressing is an inseparable act *caused* by the butler and the master. In the same manner "the Son alone assumed human nature, as long as assuming human nature does not designate an action, but the state resulting from an action."[29] John Owen's perception is interesting here. He states:

> As unto *original efficiency*, [the assumption] was the act of the divine nature, and so, consequently, of the *Father, Son*, and *Spirit*. For so are all outward acts of God—the divine nature being the immediate principle of all such operations. ... As unto *authoritative designation*, it was the act of the Father. ... As unto the *term of the assumption*, or the taking of our nature unto himself, it was the peculiar act of the person of the Son.[30]

---

27. Catherine Mowry Lacugna, "Re-Conceiving the Trinity as the Mystery of Salvation" *SJT* vol 38, no. 1 (1985): 7

28. Vidu, "Trinitarian Inseparable Operations and the Incarnation," 112.

29. Ibid., 113.

30. *Works*, 1:225. I owe this quote to Tyler Wittman's work, Tyler R. Wittman, "The End of the Incarnation: John Owen, Trinitarian Agency and Christology," *IJST* 15, no. 3 (July 2013): 298.

The end of the incarnation is ascribed to the Son, but it is clear that in the operation that is concerned with taking human nature, the entire Trinity is involved.

INVISIBLE AND VISIBLE MISSIONS

It is natural and easy to recognize the visible missions of the Trinity. The Son is sent into the world and the Spirit comes as a dove. These visible manifestations are not alone, however, as they are also accompanied by invisible missions. The invisible missions are "the sending of a divine person to a human being (or angel) through visible grace and it 'signifies a new mode of that person's indwelling, and his origin from another.' "[31] The invisible missions are, according to Thomas, connected to works of habitual grace because the sending of the Son and the Spirit into souls is not perceptible, even though the manifestation of that sending is. The perception is made visible though character transformation—new habits (or habitual grace).[32] The visible missions are "the coming of the Son of God in the flesh, and the manifestation of the Holy Spirit through visible signs (at Christ's baptism [Matt 3:13–17] and transfiguration [Matt 17:1–20], at Easter [John 20:22–23], and at Pentecost [Acts 2])."[33] Both in invisible as in the visible missions, the *taxis* is not inverted for the persons follow their processions and add created effects.

FALLENNESS AND THE OPERATIONS
OF THE TRINITY

Proper order of Trinitarian operations allows us to speak of causality and *taxis*. What does assuming a fallen human nature have to do with the inseparable operations of the Trinity? In order to answer this question, let us revisit Barth and Torrance's discussions on the *non-assumptus*.

---

31. Legge, *The Trinitarian Christology of St Thomas Aquinas*, 25.

32. For a good defense of Protestant appropriation of habitual grace, see Michael Allen, *Sanctification*, ed. Scott R. Swain (Grand Rapids: Zondervan, 2017), 246–55.

33. Gilles Emery, " 'Theologia' and 'Dispensatio': The Centrality of the Divine Missions in St Thomas's Trinitarian Theology," *The Thomist* 74, no. 4 (October 2010): 520.

KARL BARTH

For Barth, the relationship of the Trinity is key in the Gethsemane passage. This must be explained in the Trinitarian existence *ad intra* that justifies the mode of obedience of the Son in his revelation *ad extra*. This relationship of "reiteration" is so strong that tends to diminish analogical mode of thinking from the creatures. Hence, the obedience of Christ in the world is as true here as it is in God's inner reality.[34] The Gethsemane episode then shows not only how Jesus is the obedient Son of God, but also how he must trust the Father to keep him from falling.

In Jesus's trust was built the fallen human nature he assumed. He had to overcome that fallenness by trusting in the Father. As has been argued previously, this does not mean that there is fallenness in God's own life but arguing for fallenness inverts Trinitarian operations by placing a kind of sanctification that is due to the Spirit. The mode of sanctification is covered under chapter 5, but what concerns us here is that the cause and *taxis* of Trinitarian agency seem to be inverted.

As discussed above, the cause of a trinitarian operation is always rooted in the unity of the essence of God. Moreover, "God creates [or we may say, provide] because he is God *and in so far as he is God.*"[35] The person-relations constitute the basis of the acts of God toward the outside. For Barth, even though there is a presupposition of the antecedent life of the Son who positively affirms the sinlessness of Christ, Barth quickly qualifies it by stating that such thing is only a presupposition. The reality is that the electing grace, as it is repeated in the incarnation, is repeated with empowerment (ἐξουσία) in sanctification. "He receives power."[36] This kind of power received in history has been described in church history as fitting to the Spirit.

Note that there is nothing wrong in relating the Spirit to Christ in the incarnation. As we have been reminded, the incarnation is caused by the Trinity in inseparable fashion. The issue arises when Barth relates the agency of Spirit separately than that of the Son. The Son is not empowered in a vacuum, so to speak. The Spirit's action in Christ is always and

---

34. See *CD* IV/1, 178–202.
35. Emery, *The Trinitarian Theology of St. Thomas*, 341, emphasis added.
36. *CD* IV/2, 96.

everywhere also caused by the Son himself with the Father. This is a corollary of the *filioque*—the Spirit comes forth from the Father and of the Son. Each divine mission "includes and discloses the eternal procession upon which is founded."[37] Therefore, the receiving of the Spirit's power in the sanctification of Christ cannot be divorced from Christ's own breathing forth of the Spirit in his own human nature.

Furthermore, for Barth, the continuity of the hypostatic unity rests in the work of the Spirit sanctifying Christ. Moreover, "He did not sin, because from this origin He lived as a man in this true human freedom—the freedom for obedience—not knowing or having any other freedom."[38]Although Barth pays some lip service to the personal origin of the Son as a constitution of resulting sinlessness, this cannot be the determining factor for the history of the man Jesus. His humanity is fully dependent on true obedience *via* the grace of the Spirit.

As Barth prepares to discuss the *communicatio naturarum* (which as I have shown previously, ends up heading with the *communicatio gratiarum*; contrary to the tradition) he sets the stage with a brief Trinitarian theology of the incarnation.[39] It is true, he says, that the Son of God does not exist in isolation during the incarnation. Furthermore, "the three divine modes of existence are to be distinguished, but they cannot be separated."[40] Because the Son is always and everywhere present, the Trinity is there also. So, in Barth's account, the man Jesus is sustained by the Father's blessing and his "Yes" and "impelled inwardly by the comfort and *power* and direction of the Holy Spirit."[41] The Trinitarian setup presented here is used to discard any notion that Christ's humanity is deified. Christ's humanity does not become the fourth person of the Trinity, but the humanity he assumes takes the full share and participation in creation, as the Son takes full share in the deity.

Hence, the determination of the human essence assumed by the Son in obedience and sinlessness is not a naked reality, but it is the Godhead who surrounds Jesus like a garment (something external to the condition of

---

37. Legge, *The Trinitarian Christology of St Thomas Aquinas*, 89.

38. *CD* IV/2, 93.

39. *CD* IV/2, 94–97.

40. *CD* IV/2, 94.

41. *CD* IV/2, 94. Emphasis added.

Jesus).[42] This position, however, yields a rejection of any *inward* disposition of the Son caused by himself or by a classical notion of Thomistic missions. Barth himself asserts (probably with Thomas in mind) that "there can be no transferred condition, or an infused habit in this grace addressed to him."[43] For Barth, there can be no permanent *state* of blessing, since Christ comes in history and encounters us anew.

As stated above, if we follow Thomas's concepts of invisible missions as a corollary of the *opera trinitatis ad extra indivisa sunt,* then the *inward* disposition of the Son is breathed out from himself with the Spirit yielding a certain disposition and state of blessing.[44] This is because the Spirit is sent by the Son into himself and that invisible mission is consistent with the work of the Spirit who comes as the perfecter and finisher of something started by the Father and the Son. This does not mean that the Son does an incomplete job in assuming human nature. It is paramount to keep in mind the Thomistic notion of act: that an act is caused by the three persons (but does not have three different causes), even if there is one person who is considered the *terminus* of such action. This invisible, perfecting, and sanctifying work of the Spirit is then "part" of the divine cause of the Son's assumption.

T. F. TORRANCE

As seen in chapter 3, Torrance's avoidance of any dualistic notions of the atonement motivated his rejection of what he termed the Latin heresy. For Torrance the understanding of the incarnation not as "God *in* man, but God *as* man, implies a rejection of the idea that the humanity of Christ was merely instrumental in the hands of God."[45]

The way Torrance builds upon the mystery of the incarnation is inherently Trinitarian. Hence the emphasis on the fact that we must contemplate Jesus as we contemplate the divine activity: with "the [patristic] *being*-of-God-in-his-acts and the Reformation emphasis on the *acts*

---

42. *CD* IV/2, 94

43. *CD* IV/2, 94

44. For Barth's actualism, see Paul Nimmo, "Actualism" in *The Westminster Handbook to Karl Barth*, ed. Richard E. Burnett (Louisville, KY: Westminster John Knox, 2013), 1–3.

45. Torrance, *The Trinitarian Faith*, 150.

of God-in-his-being."[46] Any separation between this emphasis, and we
return to the Latin heresy. The structure of the Trinitarian argument is
as presented below.

First, the *homoousios* doctrine of the Nicene fathers forbade any dualistic separation of who the Son is in himself (in Trinitarian life) and his
revelation as Jesus of Nazareth (remember, "there is no God behind the
back of Jesus Christ"). Hence, union with God "in and through Jesus Christ
who is of one and the same being with God belongs to the inner heart of
the atonement."[47] Therefore the incarnation represents the lifting up of
humankind to the inner life of the Trinity because humankind is *homoousios* with Christ, who is *homoousios* with God.

Second, this unity between God and humankind is *real*. The term here
is being used in its technical form. Meaning at the incarnation "*God sent
his own Son in the concrete likeness of sinful flesh* (ἐν ὁμοιώματι σαρκὸς
ἁμαρτίας), and as sacrifice for sin, condemned sin in the flesh."[48] Torrance
continues pressing the issue by thinking that in this unity, Christ took what
was ours and imparted to us what was his. This *real* and ontological union
places the incarnation at center stage (even if it is not *in toto*) of the soteriological work. The "incarnational assumption of our human nature was at
the same time reconciling, healing, sanctifying and recreating activity."[49]

Third, this work of sanctification and healing is only connected to our
side of the equation. Our persons need sanctification, whereas Christ's
person does not need any, and as such, even our persons are only derivatively persons. The Spirit gave the Son his uncreated human person, so to
speak, and we are *persons personata* whereas Christ is *persona personans*.[50]
Against dualism, Torrance claims that Christ's Spirit-given-uncreated
person personalizes our created persons. Because we are persons but are
not sincere and hypocrites, we tend to live dual personal lives. The Word
personalizes us by taking out insincerity and living in full sincerity.[51]

---

46. Torrance and Walker, *Incarnation*, 85.
47. Torrance, *The Trinitarian Faith*, 159.
48. Ibid., 160.
49. Ibid., 162.
50. Ibid., 230.
51. Torrance, *The Mediation of Christ*, 69.

Some issues pointed out by Torrance are worthy and commendable; some, however, are questionable. First, when we talk about humankind being lifted up to the Trinitarian life of God, caution is advised. Appealing to the doctrine of inseparable operations is helpful in this dialogue, for the participatory aspect is made possible by the Spirit's engrafting of humankind into the life of God *via* union with Christ.

The soteriological processes of engrafting, sanctifying, and elevating human nature are fundamentally Trinitarian, and as such, they follow a certain order and principle of cause. The exchange described by Torrance ("incarnational assumption of our human nature was at the same time reconciling, healing, sanctifying and recreating activity"[52]), where the Son gives us what is his and we give him what is ours tends to attribute to the Son a work fitting in order to the Spirit. As Billings notes, the restoration is in "Christ through the Spirit as the believer grows to be 'conformable' to God; this process is culminated in the participation in Christ's resurrection and glorification, and in a beatific vision."[53] The Son sends the Spirit to us who engrafts us into the Son in a mystical union.[54] The *duplex gratia* of the Spirit's work (justification and sanctification) is manifested in one's continual growth, culminating in the beatific vision. It is true that the Spirit is involved in both ends of the *duplex* gratia, but Torrance's scheme of "objective salvation"—making one already present in Christ by the sheer fact of participating in the same human nature—tends to devalue the subjective growth in the beatific vision propelled by the Holy Spirit. Mark Garcia makes an important contribution here by reminding us of one of the qualitative differences between the personal union of the Son with a particular, human nature, and our engrafting in him:

> Unlike what is in view in the christological *communicatio* model, the union of Christ with the believer is not a hypostatic union. In our union with Christ, as Calvin repeatedly insisted, there is a union of persons in the bond of the Spirit—a union, then, of a different

---

52. Torrance, *The Mediation of Christ*, 69.

53. Billings, "United to God through Christ," 320.

54. Language borrowed from Calvin: "That joining together of Head and members, that indwelling of Christ in our hearts—in short, that mystical union—are accorded by us the highest degree of importance, so that Christ, having been made ours, makes us sharers with him in the gifts with which he has been endowed." Calvin, *Institutes* 3.11.10.

order. The Reformed Orthodox were wisely sensitive to this point, including in their discussions of the *unio mystka* or *unio spiritualis* the added qualifier sive praesentiae gratiae tantum ("by the presence of grace alone") in order to distinguish saving union with Christ from the hypostatic union of natures in the person of Christ.[55]

Any talk about participation must tread carefully both in its Trinitarian and metaphysical implications. Mark Garcia exemplifies that here by reminding us of the different order in which we participate in the Son's own life. Attributing the kind of participation that Torrance does will make the Son the *terminus* of the divine activity in sanctification. And as it is clear scripturally and theologically, sanctification (habitual or progressive) is a work of the Spirit (1 Pet 1:2; Rom 8:13).

Second, the kind of incarnational soteriology emphasized by Torrance seems to lend a hand to a diminishment of a robust Trinitarian soteriology. Kevin Vanhoozer puts the question in a masterful way: "is soteriology (i.e., participation in Christ) simply ontology writ large (i.e., a matter of partaking in human nature), as if being human were itself a sufficient condition for being 'in Christ'?"[56] There is a tendency in Torrance to overshadow everything in light of the incarnation. This move has raised questions, for years, as to whether Barth, but especially Torrance were universalists. The answer by both theologians and their interpreters has not satisfied; staying at a mere agnosticism about the possibility of universal salvation, but never rising to certainty. This discussion might seem like it has no resemblance to talk about inseparable operations. However, making soteriology, as a whole, subservient to the incarnation leads to a certain kind of divine action. This action displaces the Spirit's life in participation. If participation is merely achieved by sharing humanity with Christ, then regeneration loses its Spirit-giving facet.

Third and finally, it is unclear how is that Christ gives us our persons but heals our nature. The issue at stake here is fundamentally a person-nature

55. Mark A. Garcia, "Imputation and the Christology of Union with Christ: Calvin, Osiander, and the Contemporary Quest for a Reformed Model," *WTJ* 11 n. 4 (Fall 2006): 248.

56. Kevin Vanhoozer, "From 'Blessed in Christ' to 'Being in Christ'" in *In Christ in Paul: Explorations in Paul's Theology of Union and Participation*, ed. Michael J. Thate, Kevin J. Vanhoozer, and Constantine R. Campbell (Grand Rapids: Eerdmans, 2018), 18.

distinction. The entirety of human existence has been affected by sin (person and nature), but when Torrance speaks of the Spirit giving the Son his uncreated human person, we have to ask why is the Spirit initiating something in the divine activity?[57] As John Owen states, the Spirit's role is of "concluding, completing, perfecting acts."[58] That is because as stated earlier in this chapter, "God creates because he is God *and in so far as he is God.*"[59] The divine person *is* involved in the external relation to the world in the manner in which he is God or, again, "the eternal processions are the cause and the rationale of the making of creatures."[60]

CONCLUDING THOUGHTS ON INSEPARABLE OPERATIONS AND THE *NON-ASSUMPTUS*

The foundation laid out here sets the tone for divine actions. We must emphasize again that God acts not contrary to who he is in himself. So our discussions in the next chapter about grace, the way that God gives grace to his creation (including Jesus's own humanity), must not contradict the blessedness of his own life.

The relationship of Jesus's humanity and his divine person are non-competitive. Because God is not in this *genus* and is not being like creatures are being, the relationship he establishes with his creations must not be thought as cooperating or competing with his own blessed life. As Henk Schoot stated, "God is not different within a certain genus, on the basis of a common similarity. ... God is 'outside' of any genus, and thus God is not different from creatures the way in which creatures mutually differ. God differs differently."[61] God's simplicity stands as the background both of God's oneness and as basis for his relationship to the world as one who does not need anything even when he unites himself to humankind. Being different even in the way that he differs from humankind, God can unite himself to another nature following the fitting order in which he is himself, but even in that not change his own being. As Tanner stated,

---

57. Torrance, *The Trinitarian Faith*, 230.

58. *Works*, 4:94.

59. Emery, *The Trinitarian Theology of St. Thomas*, 341, emphasis added.

60. I *Sent* d. 14, q. 1, a. 1.

61. Kathryn Tanner, *Jesus Humanity and the Trinity* (Minneapolis, MN: Fortress Press, 2001), 12.

"Only what is not a kind—and therefore not bound by the usual differences between natures—can bring together in the most intimate unity divinity and humanity."[62]

The proposals of Christ's assumption of a fallen flesh could be corrected by applying not only the concept of inseparable operations but the Thomistic apparatus behind it. By doing this, these proposals would be less prone to buy into a fallen position at the risk of inverting Trinitarian order. It is clear from the descriptions above that by stating fallenness in Christ's flesh, the invisible missions of the persons of the Trinity do not follow the visible. Since Christ needs to receive sanctification that does not come necessarily through the presence of the divine Son in that human body/soul, but through the Spirit's power from keeping him from sinning, then the Spirit's action seems to be independent from the Son's own sending. Keeping with the axiom that what happens inside the life of God is not contradicted in the outside, we need to reject the fallen position on that basis.

---

62. Ibid., 11.

5

GRACE OF UNION
AND HABITUAL GRACE

INTRODUCTION

It is my intention here to show that the scholastic use of "grace of union" and "habitual grace" advance an important theological safeguard in Christology, especially when discussing the possibility of fallenness in Christ. Grace of union is the term used by the Scholastics (such as Thomas Aquinas and John Owen) to describe how there were no merits that preceded the union of the person of the Son with his human nature. Owen defines this grace as a unique dignity of Christ's human nature not shared with any other human being.[1] Moreover, Owen ties it to the work of the person of the Son, who graciously renders the human nature of Christ "glorious and amiable unto believers."[2] For in this notion, the human nature of Christ receives logical priority over all other created realities. Habitual grace is the grace God disposes to the soul of humankind in order for humankind to be sanctified. This grace "pertains to all saints insofar as they receive sanctifying grace from God. As such it is something created and finite which elevates the spiritual creature to share truly but imperfectly in the life of God."[3]

In order to do that I will first discuss the metaphysics of the incarnation. How did the church arrive at a robust relationship of the Son with a human nature within the entire matrix of the relationship of nature and grace? In this section I will depend heavily both on Thomas Aquinas, Herman Bavinck, and their interpreters' development of this paradigm.

---

1. *Works*, 1:227–28.

2. Ibid., 1:228.

3. Thomas Joseph White, *The Incarnate Lord: A Thomistic Study in Christology* (Washington, DC: The Catholic University of America Press, 2016), 87. cf. *ST* III. Q 7, A. 11.

Second, with the help of Thomas Aquinas, I will discuss the nature of grace of union and then of habitual grace and whether or not Christ had habitual grace. Finally, I will demonstrate how the sanctification of Christ within this Reformed-Thomistic framework does not allow for fallenness to be introduced in the human nature assumed by the Son.

THE PERENNIAL DEBATE OF GRACE
VS. NATURE AND ITS RELATIONSHIP
TO THE INCARNATION OF THE SON

Whatever it may be said of the relationship of God and the world, it has to be understood in God's free will to be in relationship with his creation. A human person, as a created being, has a *telos* given by God.[4] The debate that emerged, especially in Roman Catholic circles at mid-twentieth century, was whether humankind had an intrinsic desire to be in relationship with God (hence, this position was termed "intrinsicism") or if humankind was created in a pure form and the grace of God elevates this form (hence, a position called "extrinsicism").

For a long time after Thomas, interpreters of his theology assumed a form of pure nature that was explicitly extrinsic. It was with Maurice Blondel and his work *L'Action* that things began to shift. Blondel argued that "it is not outside of man, but within him, that we must look for the secret judgement of eternity."[5] Although the work of Blondel did not get much traction at the time because he was a philosopher and not a theologian, Henri de Lubac popularized Blondel's project in the realm of theology. For de Lubac the extreme distinction between the pure nature of humankind and the supernatural (*Surnaturel*) does not explicate humankind's innate desire for the beatific vision. In fact, the supernatural is not

> something adventitious, something "superadded" such as may have
> been the "supernatural gifts" attributed to humankind while it was
> still in the state of innocence; yet it 'dignifies' humanity much more
> than these did; it raises humanity much higher still above the level

---

4. This *telos* does not make God obligated to give humankind its completion. For even if all people have a desire to see God, this kind of creation is still dependent on God's sustenance and nature. So, in a sense, God is only compelled by himself and his own nature.

5. Maurice Blondel, *Action : Essay on a Critique of Life and a Science of Practice* (Notre Dame, IN: University of Notre Dame, 1984), 340

of its own *essence,* since it is entirely out of proportion with that essence. Finally, the supernatural must not be defined solely by its characteristic of gratuitousness; and yet it is infinitely more gratuitous than any other kind of favour could possibly be, and infinitely surpasses the *necessities [exigences]* of any possible nature.[6]

But the natural-supernatural distinction in de Lubac serves only as a backdrop for the concept of nature and grace. Grace is in the creature himself already inclining its nature to the divine. "[T]he desire of humanity for God is the result of divine action, whether by participation and imitation due to grace, *or—what amounts to the same activity—through ongoing dialogue of the soul with God.*"[7] G. W. Parker explains:

> Nature and grace for de Lubac can be elucidated in three points. Firstly, de Lubac believed that humans were created for communion with God and therefore had a natural inclination to desire God. Secondly, nature and grace are unique in that they are both a gift from God, though it is necessary to distinguish them. Thirdly, the natural desire for the supernatural is incomplete without grace.[8]

As a reaction to de Lubac's reinterpretation of Thomas, several Roman Catholic theologians proposed that a pure nature must be conceived; at the risk of making the beatific vision something due to humankind by God. Feingold asserts that "the demonstration of an *elicited* natural desire for the vision of God thus manifests the great fittingness of our supernatural elevation without endangering the distinction of the two orders."[9]

Protestants might think that they have no interest in who is interpreting Thomas correctly, but popular characterizations of Thomas among Protestantism (especially in the Dutch Neo-calvinism camp) have tended to be bleak, as if Thomas held to a sort of pure state of nature apart from

---

6. David Grumett, *De Lubac: A Guide for the Perplexed* (New York: Bloomsbury Publishing, 2007), 9.

7. Ibid., 17.

8. Gregory W. Parker, "Reformation or Revolution? Herman Bavinck and Henri de Lubac on Nature and Grace," *Perichoresis* 15, no. 3 (October 1, 2017): 84.

9. Lawrence Feingold, *The Natural Desire to See God According to St. Thomas and His Interpreters* (Naples, FL: Sapientia Press Ave Maria Univ, 2004), 432. See also Thomas White, *Wisdom in the Face of Modernity: A Study in Thomistic Natural Theology* (Ave Maria, FL: Sapientia Press, 2009), 208.

grace. This is not the position of intrisicists or extrinsicists. For both positions, Thomas saw that nature has some sort of proportionality to grace. The main question was whether this desire needed to be elicited or it was immanently present in humanity.[10]

Moreover, Arvin Vos has showed that the source of confusion in Protestantism regarding this theology has its roots in late nineteenth-century Roman Catholics characterizations of textbook Thomisms and not of Thomas himself.[11] As we make our way into Herman Bavinck's interaction with grace and nature it will be clear that there are some lines of continuity and discontinuity with these understandings—especially in his missing concept of grace and Christology.

HERMAN BAVINCK AND HIS INTERPRETERS
ON GRACE AND NATURE

The intramural debate among Roman Catholics in the end of the nineteenth-century, spilling into the twentieth century, eventually made its way into the Reformed churches. Herman Bavinck is widely regarded as one who analyzed whole concepts of theology through the relationship of nature and grace. He even states that

> Every Christian must consider two factors: creation and re-creation, nature and grace, earthly and heavenly vocation, etc.; and in accordance with the different relationship in which he puts these to each other, his religious life assumes a different character. Humankind's relationship to God is determinative of his relationship to things in general. Whoever breaks the divinely appointed connection between nature and grace is led to sacrifice one to the other. Socinianism and Anabaptism, Rationalism and Mysticism are the resulting deviant paths into which the Christian goes astray.[12]

---

10. See Manfred Svensson and David VanDrunen, ed., *Aquinas among the Protestants*, (Hoboken, NJ: Wiley-Blackwell, 2017), chap 11.

11. A. Vos, *Aquinas, Calvin, and Contemporary Protestant Thought: A Critique of Protestant Views on the Thought of Thomas Aquinas* (Grand Rapids: Christian University Press, 1985), 152.

12. Herman Bavinck, *De Bazuin* XLVIII, 12 (March 23, 1900). As quoted in Jan Veenhof, *Nature and Grace in Herman Bavinck*, trans. Albert M. Wolters (Sioux Center, IO: Dordt College Press, 2006), 14. The citation of Veenhof probably needs clarification in the current Bavinck scholarship. This book is not a work on Bavinck, but it probably needs to be said that I do

Although not using the terms (extrinsic and intrinsic) Bavinck taps into the issue by noticing that in Roman Catholic thought, nature is posed as something so low that grace is needed *ut elevet et sanet*. This Neoplatonic conception of nature is eventually rejected fundamentally in a Reformed theology that sees nature as essentially good. Grace is not needed to elevate human nature because grace is not antithetical to nature, but only to sin.[13] Hence, we can say anachronistically, that Bavinck placed himself on the intrinsic side of the debate—seeing that there is no need for a superadded gift into human nature's "pure form."

Brian Mattson's excellent study, *Restored to Our Destiny: Eschatology & the Image of God in Herman Bavinck's Reformed Dogmatics*, directs the attention to Bavinck's analysis that the Spirit is not higher than the material, and it pays high dividends in Christology. Mattson's work distils Bavinck's treatment of Christology with three movements of preparation: the triune God, creation, and the history of revelation.[14] Contrary to Barthian impulses that have their starting point in Christ, Christology (although central) cannot be where the theological enterprise begins. "Although it is a mystery, the incarnation is not, for Bavinck a complete *novum*."[15] Christ comes in the context of creation and covenant; all of which presuppose the Trinitarian action of God.

These contexts set the stage for how one ought to understand the assumption of the human nature of Christ. The free gracious act to create, for Bavinck, follows God's decision to allow the fall.[16] Mattson expands on this explaining that by following this scheme, Bavinck can maintain that Adam was a type of Christ and puts creation in its appropriate context of future maturation. Christ's nature is seen then as one of the same as Adam's and even in the incarnation it is already better. For from the beginning Christ is the *telos* of Adam (even before sin). Of course, in the resurrected state, Christ's human nature is glorified, but that does not mean that in the pre-resurrected state, it is of an inferior character. Again, we must remind ourselves that one of Bavinck's main motifs is to flee from

---

not agree with Veenhof's portrait of two Bavincks. See James Eglinton, *Trinity and Organism: Towards a New Reading of Herman Bavinck's Organic Motif* (New York: T&T Clark, 2014).

13. *RD* III, 577.

14. Brian G. Mattson, *Restored to Our Destiny* (Leiden: Brill, 2011), 168.

15. Ibid., 169.

16. *RD* III, 278.

Neoplatonic dualism in which the material is of a lower grade than the spiritual. Christ's initial incarnate state (what the Reformers called the state of humiliation) *would* be on the same "level" as Adam's, for both are in the context of creation. Thus, we can say that both are in the covenant of works. Nonetheless, the personal union introduced a category that would benefit Bavinck's treatment of Christ's human nature and aid him in interacting with Thomistic notions of grace—the categories of grace of union and habitual grace. This is not to say that Bavinck misses the point completely in his anthropology and Christology. But as John Bolt states,

> While Bavinck is on surer ground in his criticism of the idea of merit in Thomas's views, a closer look at Thomas's anthropology in *ST* 1 a.95.1 makes it clear that on three crucial points there is no substantive disagreement between them. First, the creation of humanity was itself a gift of grace (Bavinck 2003–8, 2: 544). Second, in the Fall, something of the image is lost ("image" in Thomas; righteousness and holiness or the "narrow" sense of image in Bavinck) and something is retained ("likeness" in Thomas; broader sense of image in Bavinck; Bavinck 2003–8,2: 548). Third, there is a "plus" in redemption; humanity's final destiny is more than simply a return to Adams original state (Bavinck 2003–8, 2: 543–4). There is no substantial disagreement between Thomas and Bavinck on these points. Bavinck's misreading of Thomas is an uncharacteristic misstep on his part. The point we made earlier (from Arvin Vos) that late nineteenth-century critics of Roman Catholic theology were criticizing the Thomistic textbook tradition rather than Thomas himself is true here as well. Bavinck got caught up in the groundswell of Protestant unanimity where critics tended to repeat one another.[17]

These missing categories only at surface seem to contradict Bavinck's axiom that grace is not a remedy for nature but for sin. One could ask: If Jesus's nature is perfect why do we need any talk about it receiving grace? At close inspection, however, we shall note that these categories are still aligned with Bavinck's rejection of dualism and with his organic motif.

---

17. John Bolt, "Doubting Reformational Anti-Thomism," in *Aquinas Among the Protestants*, ed. Manfred Svensson and David VanDrunen (Hoboken, NJ: Wiley-Blackwell, 2017), 143.

GRACE OF UNION

Richard Muller inserts the discussion of the grace of union under the rubric of the *Communicatio Gratiarum*. In Muller's description, the communication of graces includes the grace of union which means that the humanity of Christ is elevated above all creatures by its union to the person of the Son.[18]

In Thomas's treatment of the hypostatic union he inserts the grace of union in several places. One of the first *loci* is when Aquinas asks whether the grace of union was natural to the man Christ?[19] It seems at first that it was not natural because "the union of the Incarnation did not take place in the nature, but in the Person." Moreover, it seems that "grace is divided against nature, even as gratuitous things, which are from God, are distinguished from natural things, which are from an intrinsic principle."[20] Thomas quickly asserts that

> nature designates, in one way, nativity; in another, the essence of a thing. Hence natural may be taken in two ways: first, for what is only from the essential principles of a thing, as it is natural to fire to be carried up; second, we call natural to man what he has had from his birth, according to Ephesians 2:3: We were by nature children of wrath; and Wisdom 12:10: They were a wicked generation, and their malice natural. Therefore, the grace of Christ, whether of union or habitual, cannot be called natural as if caused by the principles of the human nature of Christ, although it may be called natural, as if coming to the human nature of Christ by the causality of His Divine Nature. But these two kinds of grace are said to be natural to Christ, inasmuch as He had them from His nativity, since from the beginning of His conception the human nature was united to the Divine Person, and His soul was filled with the gift of grace.[21]

Aquinas is making the case that the grace of union is not a merit of the humanity of Christ in its own accord, but it is still natural in the sense

---

18. Richard A. Muller, *Dictionary of Latin and Greek Theological Terms: Drawn Principally from Protestant Scholastic Theology* (Grand Rapids: Baker Book House, 1985), 72.

19. *ST* III Q2. A12.

20. *ST* III Q2. A12. arg. 2.

21. *ST* III Q2. A12. s. c.

that by the unity to the divine person, the human nature of Christ *naturally* receives grace. This first point already speaks to Bavinck's worries that nature is not a "receptacle" of grace because grace's function is for forgiveness and restoration. Aquinas is careful here to assert that the human nature of Christ is filled with grace because in union with the Divine Person the humanity of Christ receives the gift of the divine personal agency (already signaling the relationship of Grace of union with the *communicatio idiomatum*). It is *via* this relationship that the nature is elevated, not because it is lowly and worse than the spiritual reality, but because in some way it participates in the divine consortium—even if only in a *predicatio verbalis*. Such a move is important because it respects the creator-creature distinction while still affirming God's free agency in creation. On this point, Bavinck even seems to agree and be even more forceful when he says that "in Christ the human nature had to be prepared for union with the person of the Son, that is, to a union and communion with God as to that which no other creature had ever been dignified."[22]

Grace, however, is not the medium of the unity. Contrary to any other human being who is saved or sanctified by grace, Christ's human nature follows a two-step sanctifying project. First, "the grace of union is the personal being that is given gratis from above to the human nature in the Person of the Word, and is the end of the assumption."[23] This is what is commonly called the *communicatio idiomatum*. The human nature of Christ does not receive predication in isolation from the person of the Son, who *an-en-hypostatically* is the agent upon this human nature. Hence, Aquinas says that the giving of the person to the human nature makes the person the *term* (or end) of this assumption. Therefore, Aquinas is stating that in the union of creature and divine we must ultimately refer to neither but rather to the person of the Word—the ultimate "I." This move becomes even clearer when Thomas asks whether the soul of Christ incorporated the Word or the divine essence. He states,

> It is not with regard to the same, that a thing moves towards, and that it is, something; for to move belongs to a thing because of its matter or subject—and to be in act belongs to it because of its form.

22. *RD* III, 192
23. *ST* III. Q6. A6. co.

So too it is not with regard to the same, that it belongs to Christ to be ordained to be God by the grace of union, and to be God. For the first belongs to Him in His human nature, and the second, in His Divine Nature. Hence this is true: Christ as Man has the grace of union; yet not this: Christ as Man is God.[24]

Second, and this will be explored later, Christ's humanity is sanctified habitually. This, however, is only as a consequent reality of the grace of union. Because the Son unites himself to a human nature, the end result is a virtuous savior.

Meditating on the extent of the grace of God, Aquinas furthers his inquiry on whether the grace of union is infinite. His response is that because the person of the Son gives the gift of unity to the human nature and the person is infinite, this grace is an infinite grace.[25] This is because the gift is not poured into any substance of the soul or body of the human nature *per se*, but because the gift is the uniting itself. This will later be contrasted with habitual grace "since it is in the soul of Christ, as in a subject, and Christ's soul is a creature having a finite capacity; hence the being of grace cannot be infinite, since it cannot exceed its subject."[26]

Let us take stock on Thomas's concepts. The grace of union is not a mystic incorporation of the human nature into the divine consortium, but it is a slightly more forceful way of articulating the *communicatio naturarum* under the rubric of the *communicatio idiomatum*. It keeps what is proper to the human nature in place (such as finitude) and what is divine in its place (such as infinitude), but communicates it all to the divine person. The Son *qua* human has this grace from the moment of conception because it is from the beginning united to the divine person, something no other creature has ever been. Moreover, this grace is not accidental because the "personal dignity of the Word made human is [not] a common accident of both humanity and divinity."[27] The union occurs in the person—a non-accidental *suppositum* who gives existence to every being. The grace of union

---

24. *ST* III. Q16. A11. ad. 2.
25. *ST* III. Q7. A11. co.
26. *ST* III. Q7. A11. co.
27. White, *The Incarnate Lord*, 86.

then is underscored by the developments of the fifth ecumenical council of the church in which the human nature of Christ does not possess a person of its own, but it is *graced* in the union with the person of the eternal Word. It is not graced humanity because it is sinful or it needs healing (answering to Bavinck's fears); it is graced because it participates in life with the Son. John Owen defines this grace even more forcefully as a unique dignity of Christ's human nature not shared with any other human being.[28] Moreover, Owen ties it to the work of the person of the Son, who graciously renders the human nature of Christ "glorious and amiable unto believers."[29]

HABITUAL GRACE

Habitual grace does not have a good reputation in some Protestant circles. Bavinck himself painted this concept as a Romanist tendency to elevate nature irrespective of sin.[30] But what exactly is habitual grace? In his development of *habitus* theory, Aquinas follows Aristotle closely by seeing human actions in the context of the pursuit of the greater good.[31] According to Christopher Cleveland, Aquinas also follows Aristotle's understanding that habits are not isolated but are *caused* by the repetition of acts.[32] Habitual grace is then the gift of God given to the soul (the mereological locus of operations) of humankind in which the

> spiritual powers (intellect and will) are united to God by knowledge and by love. Because the process of spiritual operations in the human person occurs habitually (by operations that move from capacity to capacity), the grace that enlivens these faculties is called 'habitual.' Under grace, the saints are given the capacity to move themselves freely to know and love God. Without grace given perpetually to inspire and sustain them in this, such acts are impossible.[33]

---

28. *Works*, 1:227–8.
29. *Works*, 1:228.p
30. *RD* III, 574–75.
31. See Aristotle, *Nichomachean Ethics*, 1097b20–1098a17.
32. Christopher Cleveland, *Thomism in John Owen* (Burlington, VT: Routledge, 2016), 75.
33. White, *The Incarnate Lord*, 87.

Why then ascribe this kind of grace to Christ given that he already has infinite grace given to the human nature in the hypostatic union?

In *ST* III. Q7 Thomas gives several reasons it is necessary to ascribe habitual grace to Christ. He states:

> It is necessary to suppose habitual grace in Christ for three reasons. First, on account of the union of His soul with the Word of God. For the nearer any recipient is to an inflowing cause, the more does it partake of its influence. Now the influx of grace is from God, according to Ps. 83:12: The Lord will give grace and glory. And hence it was most fitting that His soul should receive the influx of Divine grace. Second, on account of the dignity of this soul, whose operations were to attain so closely to God by knowledge and love, to which it is necessary for human nature to be raised by grace. Third, on account of the relation of Christ to the human race. For Christ, as man, is the Mediator of God and men, as is written, 1 Tim. 2:5; and hence it behooved Him to have grace which would overflow upon others, according to John 1:16: And of His fullness we have all received, and grace for grace.[34]

Let us explain these features. First, the proximity of the human soul to the divine does not correspond to any mixture of properties. Aquinas himself states that "because together with unity of person there remains distinction of natures, as stated above (Q. 2, AA. 1, 2), the soul of Christ is not essentially Divine. Hence it behooves it to be Divine by participation, which is by grace."[35] Akin to other humans who are united to Christ, the keeping of human nature *qua* human and not divine necessitates that Christ undergoes the same kind of habitual sanctification in participation by likeness. It does not mean that this grace is necessary because there is some sin; but as it is now axiomatic in Reformed circles: all benefits we have come from being united to Christ, and his human nature also benefits from this unity.

Second, given that the grace of union leans closely to a verbal predication, with some limited ontological payoff for the human nature *per*

---

34. *ST* III Q7. A1. co.
35. *ST* III. Q7. A1. ad. 1.

se, the *actual* sanctification of his human nature needs to follow what is properly common to humans. Here we must stop to reflect on the order of "graces." First, there is no time relation but a logical one, and it is wrong to consider habitual grace as logically prior to the hypostatic union (or the grace of union) as it to cause the personal union. Such move would only thread closely to Barth's formulation as seen before. On this point Aquinas reserves an entire section in *ST* III. Q7. 13. Here, Thomas quickly connects the giving of habitual grace with the giving of the Holy Spirit himself because just as habitual grace is a power of the soul in charity, so the Spirit is one called Love/Charity. Such move tracks closely, for Thomas, with the order of the divine missions. He writes, "Now the mission of the Son is prior, in the order of nature, to the mission of the Holy Spirit, even as in the order of nature the Holy Spirit proceeds from the Son, and love from wisdom."[36] Hence, the grace of personal union precedes habitual grace because God's actions in time cannot contradict his life *ad intra.* It can be inferred that the proximity clause is not a substantial transference of grace, but the appropriation of the Son who himself sends the Holy Spirit into the human soul.

Second, it is both by seeing grace of union as a corollary of the *an-en-hy-postatic* distinction and the habitual grace as the specific mission of the Spirit (in that order) that we can avoid Bavinck's fears that grace is juxtaposed to nature instead of sin. Instead, Thomas is describing the incarnation in the proper context of the history of revelation where God acts graciously toward his creatures—including a human nature.[37]

EXCURSUS ON HEBREWS 2–5

These theological reflections are built upon important exegetical constructions. Several texts bespeak of Christ's growth in knowledge and grace. Due to the book of Hebrews' framework of Christ's solidarity and learned obedience, an elaborated interaction with Hebrews is deemed necessary.

The text of Hebrews starts with the author's affirmation of the Son's perfect imaging of the Father (1:3). He is superior to angels (1–2), Moses

---

36. *ST* III. Q7. A13. co.

37. These same moves are done by Bavinck in *RD* 2565-ff. See also Mattson, *Restored to Our Destiny,* 180–201.

(3:1–6), and any other created thing, but his superiority does not hinder him from taking our human nature and with that sympathize with us in every way.

As early as Hebrews 2:10–11, the author states: "for it was fitting that he, for whom and by whom all things exist, in bringing many sons to glory, should make the founder of their salvation perfect through suffering. For he who sanctifies and those who are sanctified all have one source. That is why he is not ashamed to call them brothers." Just after the affirmation of the suffering of Christ, the author links Jesus to other men *via* their common source. The oneness of Jesus and men, according to Peter O'Brien, could refer to their one bloodline or one common ancestor. O'Brien, however, clarifies it by pointing to God as the referent of *one source*: "Christ was uniquely the Son of God (1:2, 5), and others are sons in an extended sense (2:10)."[38] O'Brien seems partially correct here, for one can also make sense of this oneness in God by the fact that Jesus's humanity and ours are both created realities. God is the creator of all humanity, including Christ's. The Father's claim as creator of Christ's humanity furthers the argument of verse 11 by claiming Jesus's brotherhood with men and women in general.

Therefore, the suffering of Jesus is set in the context of the created human nature. This is different than the Nestorianism in which an action would be performed by the human or by the divine persons. Rather, the position described here sets the Son suffering *qua* human. His brotherhood is affirmed with us in that even the Son of God suffers in and through a created human body.

The author continues in verse 14–17: "Since therefore the children share in flesh and blood, he himself likewise partook of the same things, that through death he might destroy the one who has the power of death, that is, the devil, and deliver all those who through fear of death were subject to lifelong slavery. For surely it is not angels that he helps, but he helps the offspring of Abraham. Therefore he had to be made like his brothers in every respect, so that he might become a merciful and faithful high priest in the service of God, to make propitiation for the sins of the people."

---

38. Peter Thomas O'Brien, *The Letter to the Hebrews* (Grand Rapids: William B. Eerdmans, 2010), 109.

Sharing of flesh and blood (αἵματος καὶ σαρκός) and partaking of the same things (παραπλησίως μετέσχεν) explains how he is made like his brothers in every manner (κατὰ πάντα τοῖς ἀδελφοῖς ὁμοιωθῆναι). And in identifying with his brothers, the Son is not made of a lower status, but he brings this humanity into a unity that is of a different kind, all the while not changing this humanity. Michael Allen explains it:

> Here is no maneuver towards an emanationist or angelic/media-torial Christology; indeed, Hebrews 1:4–14 has excluded any such approach. This one is "very God" or "fully God," the repetition of the subject's identification ('he himself') attests to the specificity of the claim. This humanity is the Word or the Son's personal humanity. The classical dogmatic tradition has maintained this single subject Christology through the centuries;[39]

Christ's humanity is intimately connected to the personal life of the Son. Such unity pervasively relates to *every* aspect of the human nature without changing it. It is therefore no hermeneutical gymnastics to think that the Son sanctifies or heals his own assumed human nature in a primary fashion, then only secondarily to be habitually sanctified by the Spirit.

Once he reaches chapter 4, the author of Hebrews moves the argument further into a sympathy that does not equate sin. The true and full human nature assumed by the Son is weak, but sin's moral effects have no part in it: οὐ γὰρ ἔχομεν ἀρχιερέα μὴ δυνάμενον συμπαθῆσαι ταῖς ἀσθενείαις ἡμῶν, πεπειρασμένον δὲ κατὰ πάντα καθ' ὁμοιότητα χωρὶς ἁμαρτίας (4:15). Sympathy does not equate having to sin and feeling the consequences of that sin, but that whatever sin did to us in its real encounters with our souls, it did to Christ. Calvin aptly asserts:

> But it may be asked, What does he [the author of Hebrews] mean by *infirmities?* The word is indeed taken in various senses. Some understand by it cold and heat; hunger and other wants of the body; and also contempt, poverty, and other things of this kind, as in many places in the writings of Paul, especially in 2 Corinthians 12:10. But their opinion is more correct who include, together with external

---

39. Michael Allen, "Christ" in *T&T Clark Companion to the Doctrine of Sin* ed. Keith L. Johnson and David Lauber (New York: Bloomsbury T&T Clark, 2016).

evils, the feelings of the soul, such as fear, sorrow, the dread of death, and similar things. And doubtless the restriction, *without sin*, would not have been added, except he had been speaking of the inward feelings, which in us are always sinful on account of the depravity of our nature; but in Christ, who possessed the highest rectitude and perfect purity, they were free from everything vicious. Poverty, indeed, and diseases, and those things which are without us, are not to be counted as sinful. Since, therefore, he speaks of infirmities akin to sin, there is no doubt but that he refers to the feelings or affections of the mind, to which our nature is liable, and that on account of its infirmity. For the condition of the angels is in this respect better than ours; for they sorrow not, nor fear, nor are they harassed by variety of cares, nor by the dread of death. These infirmities Christ of his own accord undertook, and he willingly contended with them, not only that he might attain a victory over them for us, but also that we may feel assured that he is present with us whenever we are tried by them. Thus he not only really became a man, but he also assumed all the qualities of human nature. There is, however, a limitation added, *without sin;* for we must ever remember this difference between Christ's feelings or affections and ours, that his feelings were always regulated according to the strict rule of justice, while ours flow from a turbid fountain, and always partake of the nature of their source, for they are turbulent and unbridled.[40]

Calvin masterfully understands that "the feelings of the soul" are an internal and deeply related agony of the human nature. The sympathies of Christ for humanity are true and reach out to the core of Jesus's life. Nonetheless, he lives that life without any sin. This fountain of sinlessness is because he is "always regulated according to the strict rule of justice, while ours flow from a turbid fountain, and always partake of the nature of their source, for they are turbulent and unbridled." The proximity of the

---

40. John Calvin, *Commentary of the Epistle of Hebrews*. Trans. and ed. John Owen (Grand Rapids: Christian Classics Ethereal Library), Accessed August 31, 2018 https://www.ccel.org/ccel/calvin/calcom44.i.html

divine person to the human nature avails the sanctification of the nature according to the principles described above.

Hebrews 5 continues the pattern of suffering, but now introducing the clause of learned obedience and being made perfect. Although debated this clause ought not to impart fear of a low Christology. The author states, "Although he was a son, he learned obedience through what he suffered. And being made perfect, he became the source of eternal salvation to all who obey him, being designated by God a high priest after the order of Melchizedek." The syntax of the passage hints that the aorist τελειωθεὶς (made perfect) refers to the main verb ἐγένετο (he became). So that it is possible to read it as, "he was first made perfect and then he became. Both the death and resurrection/exaltation of Christ are viewed as one single event preceding his becoming the source of salvation."[41]

In summary, in sharing flesh and blood with us Jesus stands in solidarity with humankind. The fact that he primarily sanctifies his human nature with the antecedent life of the person of the Son does not create a separation between him and us. His created human nature is still the same as ours, and in ἐγένετο (becoming) the suffering that is all too common to humanity is also present in his life.

THE FALLEN CHRIST AND
THOMISTIC CONCEPTS OF GRACE

How can these discussions be helpful to refute any conception of Christ's assumption of a fallen nature? As it has been seen both in Barth and in Torrance, the language of healing and sanctification loom large in their theology of the *non-assumptus*. The precision brought by Thomas in the *Summa* allows us to reevaluate the claims of Christ's assumption of a fallen human nature.

KARL BARTH

As discussed in the chapter on inseparable operations, Barth is adamant that there can be no permanent *state* of blessing in Christ. This is both due to his conception of the incarnation as something dynamic and also

---

41. David L. Allen, *Hebrews*. The New American Commentary (Nashville, TN: B&H Publishing Group, 2010), 324.

to his theology of grace. Given that his dynamism was already treated at some length in chapter 2, this section will treat Barth's theology of grace and with that navigate how it is at odds with Thomas's.

In §30 Barth discusses his theology of grace under the heading of the divine love. As it is commonly known, he sets up the discussion with a disclaimer that we cannot be fair to divine love without connecting it with divine freedom. Eventually, we must move beyond the dialectic fears and choose one to start with. But that does not mean that one is necessarily superior to another.

Once he begins his discussion on divine love, Barth states that the grace of God must be seen as "the distinctive mode of God's being in so far as it seeks and creates fellowship by its own free inclination and favor unconditioned by any merit or claim in the beloved, but also unhindered by any unworthiness or opposition in the latter."[42] The dynamical life of God means that his condescension is gracious. And because God has determined to condescend from the beginning, then we must not shy from saying that God's being is grace itself even in presupposition of "the existence of opposition."[43]

This entire scheme is set in contradistinction to what Barth sees as the Roman Catholic thesis that grace is a "gift of God in which He might give or not give, or an attribute which might be imputed to Him or not imputed."[44] After all, "God is *vere et proprie gratiosus*."[45] To assert that grace is something arbitrary in the life of God only tends to a voluntaristic and static conception of God. Hence, God can only give grace in the measure that he gives himself.

As Barth gets to his more robust Christology in *CD* IV/2, he must discuss the relationship of God's own being as grace/gracious and the human nature of Christ. And it must be done in a way that does not diminish the real divinity of the man Jesus Christ and at the same time does not pose grace as an external gift given to him.

---

42. *CD* II/1, 353.
43. Ibid., 355.
44. *CD* II/1, 356.
45. Ibid.

Adam Neder correctly identifies five movements in Barth's theology with the elevation of human nature in the context of his rejection of Thomistic, Lutheran, and Reformed notions. The first is that stating that human nature of Christ is elevated will inevitably lead to Docetism. As Neder states, for Barth "the deification of Jesus' human nature necessarily means its transformation into something other than human nature."[46] The second element is that elevating the human nature by grace might lend a hand to synergism, where no sovereign action of God is taken, but it must cooperate with human nature. Third, to assert any kind of elevation of the human nature of Christ will operate with a substantialist ontology that does not pay careful attention to the living history in which Jesus Christ comes to us.

Fourth and perhaps most importantly to this study is Barth's explicit rejection of *habitus* theory. For him, this is nothing more than infusion of grace.[47] And as such, again, it is deaf to the history in which Christ came, making him the subject of some substance outside of his life. Fifth, Neder states the positive case in which Barth talks about the humanity of Christ being exalted instead of deified. As stated before, in taking humanity, the one "who is primarily the Son of God"[48] humbles himself. On the other hand, the human essence is "exalted to dignity ... the glory and dignity and majesty of the divine nature."[49] This exaltation of the human essence, however, is not a deification. The exaltation *is* the elevation of human essence into the *"consortium divinitatis*, into an inward indestructible fellowship with his Godhead which He does not in any degree surrender or forfeit, but supremely maintains as He becomes man."[50] Here the immanent life of God is gloriously celebrated and protected, but once this qualification is made, Barth quickly moves back to how we identify this God. He states that from eternity the grace of God has come in the form of his election—being Emanuel—God with us. The human essence that he takes on is "a clothing

---

46. Adam Neder, *Participation in Christ* (Louisville, KY: Westminster John Knox, 2009), 65.
47. *CD* IV/2, 89–90. See also, Neder, *Participation in Christ*, 89–90.
48. Neder, Participation in Christ, 100.
49. Ibid.
50. Neder, *Participation in Christ*, 100.

which He does not put off."[51] This clothing is not deified but sanctified for its exaltation, that is, the continuity of the hypostatic union.[52]

There are some important moves that are radically different than the Thomistic tradition and must be evaluated. First, it must be stated from the start that some of Barth's objections cut through in a different metaphysical approach, and as such, one needs to choose from the beginning how to approach revelation itself. If Barth's anti-static approach is chosen, his critiques are mostly correct, but if classical theism has its turn, then there are still some points to be taken.

Is *habitus* just another word for Pelagian infusion of grace? This is hardly true since the *habitus* flows from grace of union. *Habitus* is never an isolated *theologumenon* but depends on the personal presence of the Son. The blessedness of sanctification in time (Luke 2:52) is always dependent upon the metaphysical proximity of the Son to a human nature.

If anything, Barth's scheme seems to lend a hand to Pelagian notions of infusion. As seen in chapter two and here, the continuity of the hypostatic union is dependent upon the Christ receiving power. Of course, this must be quickly qualified, as Barth is not operating with a state of blessing but with an actualistic ontology. Even so, in the end, it seems that the *communicatio naturarum* and/or *idiomatum* is subordinated to the *communicatio gratiarum*—in the living history of the man Jesus Christ. And in this formulation, the give and take between divinity and humanity seems to be awfully close to a synergistic understanding of divine operations.

This grace, in Barth's structure, sanctifies the fallen nature of Christ and serves to conceptualize the continuity of an incarnation that would otherwise not continue. The fallen human nature of Christ also articulates this actualism in which exaltation and humiliation are coextensive in "solidarity terms." In doing that, Barth needs to reject the classic scholastic successive states and hence any notion that the humanity of Christ might be "so distinct" from the Son himself that it might be in proximity to him and receive grace. Proximity *could* mean Nestorianism since it tends to downplay the language of union. We, however, need to note two important

---

51. Ibid., 101.

52. See chap. 2 of this book. The *excursus* on the Garden of Gethsemane is telling on this concept.

movements: first, the proximity clause is not independently floating in Aquinas's construction, but as demonstrated above, it is logically second-ary to the grace of union; second, Nestorianism stays close to a scheme in which some actions might be ascribed to the human Jesus because of his fallenness and some not (i.e., Barth's exegesis of the Gethsemane).

T. F. TORRANCE

As described in chapter 3, Torrance conceptualizes the *non-assumptus via theosis* and the *an-en-hypostatic* distinction. Both issues are relevant to a theology of grace, since *theosis* is used to talk about participation in general terms and the *an-en-hypostatic* distinction is a way to describe the same participation in more specific terms of union *in* Christ.

The participation resultant from *theosis* is understood as *prothesis* "divine purpose," *mysterion* "mystery," and *koinonia* "fellowship/commu-nion." We have seen that the use of *mysterion* will replace the need of a subjective response to the gospel. The union of the Son with estranged reality of fallen human nature heals, sanctifies and elevates this body of sin into the very life of God. Although I have already pointed some problems between the one and the many in this construction—Christ and the church in chapter three—I will focus on the meaning of sancti-fication for Torrance.

Because Christ assumes a fallen flesh and does not sin, this means that Jesus is unlike us, who sin, "but it also means that by remaining holy and sinless in our flesh, he condemned sin in the flesh he assumed and judged it by his very sinlessness."[53] Therefore, in the "likeness of sinful flesh, he is unlike the sinner"[54] because he does not act according to that flesh's incli-nations. As Jesus operates in that flesh as God's *being-in-act* we witness the atoning exchange taking place; for it is in that event that he "condemns sin in the flesh, its sanctification of our humanity through the gift of divine righteousness and sanctification of the man Christ."[55] The sanctification of the man Christ occurs in the mystery of the union of God and human-kind so that it predates any other human's response to what God has really

---

53. Torrance and Walker, *Incarnation*, 63.
54. Ibid.
55. Ibid.

done in Christ. What God has done in Christ is already the subjective and objective aspects of the atonement. Sanctification, because it is also part of the entire "package" of the gospel, it must be accomplished objectively and subjectively in the hypostatic union.[56] Torrance states,

> Justification by grace alone remains the sole ground of the Christian life; we never advance beyond it, as if justification were only the beginning of a new self-righteousness, the beginning of a life of sanctification which is what we do in response to justification. Of course we are summoned to live out day by day what we already are in Christ through his self-consecration or sanctification, but sanctification is not what we do in addition to what God has done in justification.[57]

Jesus remains obedient in his earthly ministry even when united to something as low as the flesh of sin.

The issue at hand must be asked in these terms: when is the hypostatic union finally complete? At first, Torrance seems categorical that when "he [Christ] enters into our lowly creaturely and fallen existence, means also the elevation of our creaturely existence."[58] But he also asserts, reflecting on the language of Hebrews, that "he learned obedience, bringing his holy relation with sinners to its perfection and completion at last on the cross."[59] It is at least confusing in Torrance's discussion. As said in chapter three, the virgin birth serves as a signpost for *theosis* which creates a difference of degree between humankind and God in its participation. Torrance states,

> The virgin birth can also not be considered in abstraction from the triumphant consummation of Christ's life in his resurrection, for it

---

56. Radcliff and Purves see sanctification as a second work to be a serious distortion of Calvin's teaching that justification and sanctification are inseparable in Christ. See Alexandra S. Radcliff and Andrew Purves, *The Claim of Humanity in Christ: Salvation and Sanctification in the Theology of T. F. and J. B. Torrance* (Eugene, OR: Pickwick Publications, 2016), 123–33. J. B. Torrance and T. F. Torrance see the Westminster Confession as shifting away from a focus on God and his work to believers and their work. In contrast, see Joel R. Beeke, *Assurance of Faith*, 2nd rev. ed. edition (New York: Peter Lang Publishing, 1994), 49–85.

57. Thomas F. Torrance, *Theology in Reconstruction* (Eugene, OR: Wipf & Stock Pub, 1996), 161–62.

58. Torrance and Walker, *Incarnation*, 59.

59. Ibid., 64.

is there that the mystery of his person is revealed. In fact the birth of Jesus of the virgin Mary and the resurrection of Jesus from the virgin tomb (where no one had ever yet been laid) are the twin signs which mark out the mystery of Christ, testifying to the continuity and the discontinuity between Jesus Christ and our fallen humanity. The incarnation is not only a once and for all act of assumption of our flesh, but the continuous personal union of divine and human nature in the one person of the incarnate Son, a personal union which he carried all the way through our estranged estate under bondage into the freedom and triumph of the resurrection. Thus it is in the resurrection that we see the real meaning of the virgin birth, while the virgin birth has much to tell us about the resurrection. These are then the twin signs testifying to the miraculous life of the Son of God within our humanity, the one at the beginning and the other at the consummation of the earthly life of Jesus.

Although this is homiletically appealing, the parallel between womb and tomb must not set the tone for the metaphysics of the incarnation. Is the incarnation really complete only in light of the resurrection or does it have a character of its own?

Again, Thomas is helpful in clarifying this issue. He asks in *the Summa Theologiae* if there were any merits that preceded the union of the incarnation. Reflecting on Luke 1:35: "The Holy which shall be born of thee shall be called the Son of God," Thomas asserts that "every operation of this man followed the union. Therefore no operation of His could have been meritorious of the union."[60] Henceforth, it is difficult to see how Torrance's couplet of womb-tomb may have any bearings on a theology of the incarnation itself. To do that will eventually place *habitus* in front of grace of union only to its own peril. At the risk of sounding repetitive, by doing this is to place the mission of the Spirit in front of the mission of the Son and therefore generating all sorts of problems for God's revelation of himself.

The *an-en-hypostasis* bespeaks of participation in two ways according to Torrance: "once for all union" and "continuous union."[61] These concepts

---

60. *ST* III. Q 2. A11. co.

61. Torrance and Walker, *Incarnation*, 85.

cannot be separated, but must be seen in constant tension during the life of Christ. Moreover, because they are always in tension, they are a clear christological manifestation that the church must reject the Thomistic static conception of divine agency and opt for a more dynamic one.

The "once for all union" has as its content the general humanity that the Son assumes in the grace of God. And it is once again reflected in the doctrine of the virgin birth. Jesus Christ came as a man under the law and therefore in continuity with our sinful existence. He is also the firstborn of the new creation and also in discontinuity with our sinful existence.[62] Hence we must not ask merely biological questions about his human nature; for to ask such questions misses the point of this gracious event in which "the virgin birth is the outward sign, the sign that here in the midst of our humanity. ... God is creatively at work a new way—the sign, in fact, that he who is born of Mary is the creator himself."[63] Moreover, the virgin birth is the sign of union between God and humankind. The sign points to the mystery of the incarnation, but the sign itself is not the reality of the incarnation. Those are all explanations in a *via negative* fashion. Torrance's positive explanations of the virgin birth states what he actually believes regarding the humanity of Jesus. First, it is a one directional movement. It is sheer grace, for no human can produce something like the virgin birth (and it is once and for all). Second, it is a recreation out of an old creation. It presupposes the existence of another creation. So, the incarnation is not *ex nihilo*, but *ex virgine*. And it is also in this sense that Christ comes into our "fallen condition in order to redeem and sanctify it."[64] For he takes the flesh of this virgin who is fallen. Third, the virgin birth is the pattern of grace. By this Torrance means that the Christian message is the Christmas message. We have nothing to do with what happened to that virgin, but it is still the good news to us.

The general humanity of Jesus is then explicated through the *an-hypostatic* notion in which the Son "is in solidarity with all humanity."[65] He did not take one man who has an independent personality, but "took possession

---

62. Ibid., 94.
63. Torrance and Walker, *Incarnation*, 95.
64. Ibid., 100.
65. Ibid., 231.

of our human nature, as to set aside that which individuates us human beings [...] to assume that which unites us with one another."[66]

The "continuous union" as *en-hypostasis* speaks of the particularity of the assumption. Here, in tension with the "once for all union," the Son "comes also as an individual human being in our humanity, seeking in addition a solidarity in terms of the interaction of persons within our human and social life, in personal relations of love."[67]

In conclusion, the use of *an-en-hypostasis* for Torrance is not so much a negative-positive affirmation of the existence of a person in the *act* of assumption (although he does make some of the same comments as it is classically affirmed)[68] as it is a conceptual maneuver to speak of assumption of humanity in general/irreducible and particular ways. In summary and in Torrance's own words:

> The *anhypostatic* assumption speaks of God's unconditional and amazingly humble act of grace in assuming our humanity in the concrete likeness of the flesh of sin. But within that, *enhypostasia* speaks of the fact that the person of Christ was the person of the obedient Son of the Father, who in his humanity remained in perfect holy communion with the Father from the very beginning, and so was sinless, and absolutely pure and spotless and holy. Thus he, the *enhypostatic* Son of Man, lived out a life of perfect and sinless obedience to the Father in the midst of the fallen human nature which he had *anhypostatically* assumed, and in virtue of which he had entered into solidarity with all mankind. But as *enhypostatic* Son of Man Jesus Christ entered deeply and acutely into personal relations with sinners, so that in personal and responsible ways of the profoundest nature, he might enter within our personal human structure of existence, and answerably the whole burden of our sin and guilt upon himself so that he, the just, was loaded with our unrighteousness and he, the holy one, was loaded with our guilt that he in our place and on our behalf might expiate sin and guilt

---

66. Ibid., 231.
67. Torrance and Walker, *Incarnation*, 231.
68. Ibid., 228–29.

and make propitiation for us before the Father, thus restoring us
to the Father in purity and truth and love.[69]

The fact that, for Torrance, Jesus sanctifies us by acting within that
human nature (in full solidarity with us) may imply that the union with
humankind is of the same kind humankind has with him in salvation.
Noteworthy even is Torrance's language of sanctification. Humankind
is objectively and subjectively sanctified because of unity with vicarious
humanity of Christ.

As a response to these reformulations we may retrieve Aquinas's explanation that the difference of the union in Christ is of kind and not degree
(as Torrance seemed to suggest in his account of sanctification). Aquinas's
work in *Summa Contra Gentiles* assumes that the human nature, instead of
being a proper and common feature between Christ and other humans,
is an instrument of the Son.[70] Thomas compares the instrumentality of
human nature assumed to a hand in someone's body: "man's hand is an
instrument united and proper to him, whereas the spade is distinct from
him and common to many."[71] The hand is united to the body, but it is not
the same kind of unity that the spade has with the body.[72]

When Torrance plays with *an-en-hypostasis* as to speak of assumption of
humanity in general/irreducible and particular ways, he may have created
a space for the gracious event of the incarnation to become conditioned
upon the "final sanctification" of Christ. In doing this, he places *habitus*
theory as at least logically equivalent, or in an unnecessary tension with
grace of union. For as Aquinas said, "the mission of the Son is prior, in the
order of nature, to the mission of the Holy Spirit, even as in the order of
nature the Holy Spirit proceeds from the Son, and love from wisdom."[73] If
the final sanctification, via the new theologizing of *enhypostasis* as continuous union, is held even in tension with the new theologizing of *anhypostasis*

---

69. Ibid., 232.

70. *SCG*, IV, c. 41.

71. Ibid.

72. Ibid. "Accordingly Christ's human nature is compared to God as a proper and
united instrument, as the hand is compared to the soul."

73. *ST* III. Q7. A13. co.

in sanctification, then the mission of the Spirit and of the Son follow no order and are also in some kind of confusing tension.

CONCLUDING THOUGHTS ON GRACE OF UNION, HABITUAL GRACE, AND THE *NON-ASSUMPTUS*

In former times, *habitus* theory was basically synonymous to Pelagianism. Such presentations have warrant, especially if one sees Thomists who have ran too far with Thomas's theology. As seen in this chapter, however, if proper Trinitarian life is in place and the order of action is respected, then *habitus* is never divorced from grace of union in Christology.

Sanctification and grace must be placed in their proper theological framework. The common conception that sanctification is the work of the spirit is a good direction, but it does not locate sanctification in its entire theological setting. How we talk about sanctification must respect the mode of God's action. The Spirit is the end of the work in which sanctification is located, but this same work is authored by the Father and acted on by the son.

Those who advocate for the fallen human nature of Christ, necessitate a kind of sanctification that achieves some kind of final union at the end of Christ's life. By placing the emphasis on the progressive/habitual character of this sanctification in Christ, without actually paying close attention to the preceding sanctification of the personal presence of the Son, the advocates of the *non-assumptus* have not only forgotten important categories, but have also dislocated the action of the Spirit in relation to the Son.

6

ORIGINAL SIN

Original sin is a convoluted term that serves many purposes to many people. From Augustine's debate with Pelagius to the mature theology of John Owen and Francis Turretin, much has happened. Although it would be fascinating to visit Augustine's doctrine of original sin, I will briefly discuss it only when some of the Post-Reformers discussed here also do it. Here, I will prove that the Post-Reformation doctrine of original sin offers a robust tool to refute any notion of assumption of fallenness in Christ's human nature.

Since the Post-Reformation relied heavily on John Calvin's theology, I will deal with a recent treatment of Calvin's doctrine of original sin and its relationship to Christ. R. Michael Allen points to Calvin's doctrine of original sin in order to argue for Christ's assumption of a fallen human nature within a matrix of doctrines.[1] I will first present Allen's arguments in context. Second, I will evaluate Allen's proposal and suggest a more faithful reading of Calvin's doctrine of original sin. Third, I will interact with Calvin's use of sanctification in Christ. Fourth, I will retrieve some Post-Reformed understandings of original sin (principally from the neo-calvinist Herman Bavinck) as a way to comprehensively see the assumption of humanity both in its natural state as also in the Trinitarian component. Bavinck's organic motif provides a certain explanation that helpfully avoids the charges of arbitrariness in the doctrine of imputation. Finally, I will evaluate Barth and Torrance's proposal of the *non-assumptus* in light of

---

1. R. Michael Allen, "Calvin's Christ: A Dogmatic Matrix for Discussion of Christ's Human Nature." *International Journal of Systematic Theology* 9, no. 4 (October 2007): 382–97. Allen's article has been fairly influential in Calvin scholarship and continues to be used to support a certain reading of Calvin. See also R. Michael Allen, *The Christ's Faith: A Dogmatic Account* (New York: Bloomsbury T&T Clark, 2009), chap. 3, pt. 3. Ho-Jin Ahn, "The Humanity of Christ: John Calvin's Understanding of Christ's Vicarious Humanity," *SJT* 65, no. 2 (2012): 145–58.

the Post-Reformed doctrine of original sin, its development, and improvement of Calvin's doctrine.

CALVIN'S CHRIST OR ALLEN'S CALVIN: A CRITICAL APPRECIATION OF R. MICHAEL ALLEN'S DEPICTION OF CALVIN'S CHRISTOLOGY

Calvin's (1509–1564) doctrine of original sin is anything but simple. Especially when one tries to read Calvin through later Reformed categories, Calvin's language on original sin can sound awfully Semi-Pelagian.[2] In R. Michael Allen's 2007 article "Calvin's Christ: A Dogmatic Matrix for Discussion of Christ's Human Nature," he asserts that Calvin's view on the transmission of original sin entails no imputation of guilt. In what follows, I will outline the pertinent sections of Allen's argument so that I can interact with the possibility or not for Christ to assume a fallen human nature.

Allen starts by asserting that in Calvin's definitions of original sin he only refers to depravation and corruption, but not guilt—imputed or biologically transmitted. Due to the reticence of the fathers of the church to talk about original sin with clarity, the error of Pelagius surfaced. Therefore, Calvin proceeds to refute the Pelagian mistake that original sin propagates only by imitation.[3]

Next, Allen shows that Calvin treats the transmission of sin with great care both in *The Institutes* and in his Commentaries. Calvin's theology aims to show that Adam is a type of Christ that "in his action leads to the ensuing status of his people."[4] These effects on Adam's progeny mean that "the punishment of Adam's error certainly affects the constitution of all

---

2. The Semi-Pelagian view of transmission of sin is that Adam's sin entails corruption but *not* an imputation of guilt. Fesko asserts that "this view has been historically associated with Josua Placaeus (1596–1655). Placaeus believed that humanity was guilty because they sinned; they did not sin because they were guilty. Is humanity's guilt antecedent or consequent? The main thrust of his argument is that humanity does not inherit Adam s guilt but a corrupt nature, and this corrupt nature leads them to sin." See J. V. Fesko, *Death in Adam, Life in Christ: The Doctrine of Imputation* (Fearn, Scotland: Mentor, 2016), 212. For Calvin one is already guilty even before he acts. He does not have a category for a straight imputation of Adam's guilt, but he understands humans to be guilty because of the obnoxious nature we inherit from Adam.

3. Calvin, *Institutes* 2.1.5–10.

4. Allen, "Calvin's Christ," 386.

descendants."[5] Calvin avoids speculative talk on the mode of transmission (whether by imputation or not), but tracks closely to the biblical language of "effects."[6] So Allen concludes, "[y]et again Calvin has noted the inheritance of a depraved, corrupted nature—referring to this despoiling as original sin. The natural gifts were destroyed with the fall from moral rectitude; the supernatural gifts were severely corrupted (though not destroyed). Calvin quite emphatically distances himself from the Pelagian impulse found in contemporaries such as Servetus."[7]

On the other side, for Allen, having successfully demonstrated that imitation is not a properly biblical category for transmission of sin, the necessary consequence of Calvin's definition of original sin is that depravity and guilt are not necessary bedfellows. Calvin completely refrains from associating the word guilt with his definitions of original sin "always and everywhere."[8] An example is given in the following quote:

> Adam, by sinning, not only took upon himself misfortune and ruin but also plunged our nature into like destruction. This was *not due to the guilt of himself alone, which would not pertain to us at all,* but was because he infected all his posterity with that corruption into which he had fallen.[9]

In this section, Calvin seems to consider guilt non-transferable from Adam to us. Allen continues to expound that, in the immediate context of the aforementioned quote, Calvin proves guilt to be a reality of every human being after Adam, so much so, that we are by nature children of wrath (Eph 2:3). Having shown, however, that guilt does not appear in Calvin's definition of original sin, but is present in Adam's seed, Allen does not find Calvin's comments here decisive to say that guilt is imputed. He

---

5. Ibid.

6. So Allen appeals to Calvin's definition of original sin in his commentary on Psalm 51: "It is enough that we hold, that Adam, upon his fall, was despoiled of his original righteousness, his reason darkened, his will perverted, and that, being reduced to this state of corruption, he brought children into the world resembling himself in character." *Commentary* on Psalm 51:5.

7. Allen, "Calvin's Christ," 387.

8. Ibid. Allen's survey of Calvin's doctrine to original sin is thorough. The works of Calvin that he explores are: *The Institutes* 2.1, Commentary on Romans 5, Commentary on Genesis 3, and Commentary on Psalm 51.

9. Calvin, *Institutes* 2.1.6. Emphasis added.

concludes then that for Calvin we are guilty because "ethics encompasses something of a 'judgement by context' "[10]

What exactly is "judgement by context"? Allen responds, "God sees the entire context of the life to be lived by a fetus and, on the basis of the sinful context to come, pronounces that fetus' present existence within the womb as sinfully guilty."[11] Therefore, as it is certain that one will express his own depravity in time, he is deemed guilty even from the moment of conception.[12] For Calvin, Allen affirms again, guilt is not passed from Adam to other members of humanity. The lack of judicial tones in any formulation of Calvin's definition of the doctrine of original sin conclusively renders him outside of the traditional accounts of this doctrine.[13]

This account certainly seems to overthrow the direct parallel between Adam and Christ. Indeed, it does not reflect the later Scholastic treatment of the doctrine. Allen suggests, however, that whereas Calvin has a one-step relationship in the case of Christ and believers (the imputation of Christ's righteousness), he has a two-step relationship from Adam to humanity (the inheritance of a sinful nature that then becomes guilty due to its own actions, but is imputed before time due to God's foreknowledge).

Because the inheritance of a corrupted nature is different than judgment of guilt, Allen announces that Christ's assumption of a fallen human nature would not render him liable to punishment. Since Christ's

---

10. Allen, "Calvin's Christ," 388.

11. Allen laments that "[u]nfortunately, documentation of the particular way in which foreknowledge operates in Calvin's system is beyond the limits of this article. Suffice it to say that Calvin, by positing a 'contextual judgement' whereby even the existence of a fetus is found to be sinful, does not contradict his insistence on predestination as based on God's sovereign decree, rather than upon his foreknowledge of human action." Allen, "Calvin's Christ," 389.

12. Allen states, "Such depravity surely brings about 'fruits of sin' continually and, in the light of Calvin's notion of 'contextual judgement,' existence itself is tainted from the point of conception." Allen, "Calvin's Christ," 389.

13. Here Allen cites Calvin's *Commentary on Romans*. Allen asserts that this is almost a definitive account in which Calvin rejects any imputation of guilt. " 'Paul is not dealing here with actual sin,' for that is later consequential to each person's doing. When Paul notes that 'by the trespass of one, the many have died' (Rom. 5:15), he 'means that corruption has descended from him to us.' This is perhaps Calvin's most explicit statement regarding the sequence of events pertaining to Adam's fall and our guilt: 'It is not his fault that we perish, as though we ourselves were not to be blamed; but Paul ascribes our ruin to Adam, because his sin is the cause of our sin. By our sin I mean that which is natural and innate in us.' " Allen, "Calvin's Christ," 389.

contextual reality is one without sin, he can receive corruption—which is tendency to sin. Nonetheless, because he does not act in sin in itself, he can have a fallen/corrupt nature without being legally culpable. Questions regarding the tainting of sin in the divine are taken by Allen's account of the *Communicatio Idiomatum* that safeguards the transmission of sin to the divine nature with a hermeneutical maneuver.[14]

CALVIN'S CHRIST IN CONTEXT

What shall we say then? Is Allen correct? Here we shall evaluate his proposal and show that although he tracks closely to the vocabulary of Calvin, he fails to interpret Calvin's theology in its own context.

First, Allen is correct that Calvin does not incorporate the word "guilt" in any of his definitions of original sin. Calvin seems wary of saying that we have the fault or the guilt of Adam. He affirms that "nothing is farther from the usual view than for all to be made guilty by the guilt of one, and thus for sin to be made common."[15] Moreover, Calvin asserts that although we are justly condemned from the beginning, "this is not liability for another's transgression."[16]

Second, Allen fittingly interprets Calvin as one who avoids dogmatic speculation. In Calvin's works he rejects the word guilt or fault of Adam because it does not appear in Scripture's treatment of the two heads or types of humans. In the Bible's treatment of Romans 5 and 1 Corinthians 15, the terms used are "transgression," "sin," "trespass," and "disobedience."

---

14. "Hermeneutical" rather than "ontological" because that is Allen's purpose: "This discussion of Calvin's careful manner of discussing the relation of the two natures of Christ is not to suggest that he had no doctrine of the *communicatio idiomatum*, rather it must be noted that his discussion of the *communicatio* does not operate on the ontological level. Calvin discusses the *communicatio* within his hermeneutical discussion of New Testament texts regarding the person and nature(s) of Christ. Calvin refers to the *communicatio* as a 'figure of speech' whereby: 'They sometimes attribute to Him what must be referred solely to His humanity, sometimes what belongs uniquely to His divinity; and sometimes what embraces both natures but fits neither alone.'" Allen, "Calvin's Christ," 391. David Willis agrees: "for Calvin the *Communicatio Idiomatum* is primarily a hermeneutical tool [contrasted to an ontological one] to keep in balance the variety of scriptural witness to the one Person; but it rests upon and presupposes the hypostatic union." David Willis, "Calvin's Catholic Christology: The Function of the so-Called Extra Calvinisticum in Calvin's Theology," *Studies in Medieval and Reformation Thought*, 2 (Leiden: Brill, 1966), 67.

15. Calvin, *Institutes* 2.1.5.

16. Ibid., 2.1.8.

Third, note that Calvin's interlocutors in the *Institutes* and his *Commentary on Romans* are mainly Pelagius, Menno Simons, and the Marcionites. So, to analyze Calvin's theology of original sin, one has to keep in mind that chief among Calvin's concerns is repealing the notion of transmission by imitation.

For Calvin, this corruption of our nature is not only an inclination of our make-up. In the context of defining original sin as "a hereditary corruption and depravity ... that produces in us works which in Scripture are termed works of the flesh,"[17] Calvin asserts that this corruption is designated by Paul *as sin* and it makes us obnoxious to God. Furthermore, right after the discussion in which Calvin says that an infant suffers not for another's fault even when in the womb, Calvin claims that "their entire nature is as it were, a seed-bed of sin, and therefore cannot but be odious and abominable to God. Hence it follows, that it is properly deemed sinful in the sight of God."[18] Allen appeals to "contextual judgement" here in order to make sense of Calvin's doctrine and make it fit into the trajectory he is drawing: namely, that Christ can have a fallen human nature.

Allen's argument of two-step toward guilt—the inheritance of a sinful nature that then becomes guilty due to its own actions—depends on this notion of "contextual judgement" because Christ is able to receive a corrupted nature and not be sinful in his own context. There are two problems with Allen's approach to Calvin here. The first is that Allen never discusses the mechanism of this judgment: Is it predestination? Creation? Foreknowledge? The second is that based on Calvin's discussion, nature itself, coming from Adam, already makes you liable to punishment and is obnoxious to God. Because post-lapsarian human nature is a seedbed of sin and Paul calls it sin, then even though corruption is not the same thing as guilt, it carries with it the principle of guilt. Therefore, Christ cannot, in his human nature, be obnoxious to God.

In the Reformed tradition after Calvin, corruption and guilt are differentiated, but both come from Adam.[19] So, a fetus is guilty because Adam is

---

17. Ibid.

18. Ibid.

19. For a recent treatment, see John Murray, *The Imputation of Adam's Sin* (Grand Rapids: Eerdmans, 1959). For a classical treatment on double imputation, see Francis Turretin, *Institutes of Elenctic Theology*, vol. 1, ed. James T. Dennison Jr. (Phillipsburg, NJ: P & R Publishing,

his representative head and corruption is transmitted because the entire nature is affected. Notice that Allen is correct to say that Calvin is not in accord with this later Reformed doctrine.[20] Calvin purposefully avoids any idea of transference of guilt from Adam to his progeny. Such thing for Calvin is metaphysically and exegetically impossible.[21] Nonetheless, fallen nature is so significantly corrupted that, on the basis of its own hideousness, God pronounces it guilty. Each person's particular concrete nature actualizes guilt because it shows itself to be an instrument of ungodliness. Hence, my departure from Allen's interpretation is evident, for it is due to the condition in which one is conceived that he is guilty and not *via* his extrinsic context that is seen in advance by God. Therefore, Calvin is able to say that

> There is consequently but one way for us to interpret the statement, "We have died in Adam": Adam, by sinning, not only took upon himself misfortune and ruin but also plunged our nature into like destruction. This was not due to the guilt of himself alone, which would not pertain to us at all, but was because he infected all his posterity with that corruption into which he had fallen. Paul's statement that "by nature all are children of wrath" could not stand, unless they had already been cursed in the womb itself.[22]

We are then children of wrath by nature because of the nature we received from Adam. Allen is correct in saying that for Calvin we do not receive Adam's immediate guilt. The total corruption he plunged us in

---

1993), I.ix.9; 22;24. For a good introduction to the different approaches to the transmission of sin, see J. V. Fesko, *Death in Adam, Life in Christ: The Doctrine of Imputation* (Fearn, Scotland: Mentor, 2016), 205–20.

20.   This is contrary to popular Reformed interpretations of Calvin. Michael Horton, for example, asserts that Calvin has a doctrine of double imputation. See Michael Horton, "A Shattered Vase: The Tragedy of Sin in Calvin's Thought (1.15; 2.1-4)" in *A Theological Guide to Calvin's Institutes: Essays and Analysis, Paperback Edition*, ed. Peter A. Lillback and David W. Hall (Phillipsburg, NJ: P&R Publishing, 2015), 157.

21.   Calvin's translation of Rom 5:12 gives a clue into his logic of the relationship of Adam's sin and ours. He translates, "*Quamobrem sicut per unum hominem peccatum in mundum introiit, et per peccatum mors; atque ita in omnes homines mors pervagata est. quandoquidem omnes peccaverunt:*" The Greek clause "ἐφ' ᾧ" is translated here as the conjunction "*quandoquidem.*" *Quandoquidem* has more of a notion of a statement of fact than a causative or consequential preposition would have. Paraphrasing, his translation in English: Wherefore, as by one man sin entered into the world, and death by sin; and so death passed upon all men, with that result, all have sinned.

22.   Calvin, *Institutes* 2.1.6

deserves death—and that is condemnation.[23] Again, Allen incorrectly assumes a notion of judgement by context, instead of appealing to Calvin's notion of the hideousness of nature itself. Therefore, we can understand Calvin's *Commentary* on Romans 5:12:

---

23. Many scholars claim, contrary to Allen's proposal, that Calvin held to a classical Post-Reformed view of the transmission of sin (imputation and corruption). See Donald Macleod, *The Person of Christ* (Leicester, England: Inter-Varsity Press, 1998); Don Macleod, "Original Sin in Reformed Theology," in *Adam, the Fall, and Original Sin: Theological, Biblical, and Scientific Perspectives*, ed. Hans Madueme and Michael Reeves (Grand Rapid: Baker Academic, 2014), 129–46. I have not found scholars that described Calvin's view (except, possibly for Randall Zachman) in my terms. Henri Blocher, however, seems to have a view similar to what I described as Calvin's. He asserts, "How did punishment, death, reach all persons on the basis of ἐφ' ᾧ their actual sinning? It reached them in the same way that death entered Adam's person: since we are all in Adam, the head, sin could be reckoned to them according to the terms of the Adamic covenant, as offshoots of his sin. This is manifest in the imputation possible independently of Adam. ... The hypothesis I propose easily accounts for the imperfect symmetry between the two heads of humankind. Adam's role is more firmly cast than in the 'looser' reading of Romans 5; at the same time, the unattested and difficult thesis of the imputation of an *alien* sin is avoided—without downplaying the tragic realism of the Augustinian human predicament." Henri Blocher, *Original Sin: Illuminating the Riddle New Studies in Biblical Theology* (Grand Rapids: IVP Academic, 1997), 77, 80. Schreiner provides a good summary of Blocher's view, calling it a semi-mediative view: "Blocher rejects alien guilt, and ends up arguing that Adam as our head transmits a depraved and corrupt nature to human beings. Hence, the individual sin of human beings mirrors the sin of Adam. The upshot of Blocher's view is that human beings become guilty when they sin personally since they are not charged with guilt because of Adam's sin." Thomas Schreiner, "Adam and the Fall in Dispute," in *Adam, the Fall, and Original Sin*, 287.

Murray also seems to read Calvin's commentary on Romans 5:12 to lead into a different trajectory than the Reformed Orthodox. Although Murray is probably more sympathetic with Calvin in his description of the *Institutes* than I am. In Murray's classic work on the imputation of Adam's sin he quotes this lengthy passage from Calvin's commentary above and also points out the nature of the "*quandoquidem*" conjunction as a statement of fact and gives his verdict: "The same objections apply to this interpretation [Calvin's] as apply to the Romanist position. While it is true that Calvin is not encumbered by the difficulty Romish exegetes encounter when they are faced with the necessity of categorizing as sinful that which does not intrinsically meet the requirements of their own definition of sin and while Calvin's view of original sin is thoroughly Pauline and biblical, yet, exegetically, he has not been successful in analyzing the precise thought of the apostle in this passage. In other words, he has not been able to get above the Augustinian tradition in the exposition of Romans 5:12." Murray, *The Imputation of Adam's Sin*, 17–18. Although Murray is correct to point out that Calvin is not interpreting Romans 5:12 together with his successors, I would not innocently describe him as a mere Augustinian. The Augustinian position holds to a numerical representativity— where all humans are seminally in Adam. Calvin holds to a representative view, but even in his representativity, it is metaphysically impossible to impute guilt to his descendants. Just like Blocher, Calvin holds that the representativity of Adam wrecks the natural make up of everyone after him, but it is impossible for one to be guilty of someone else's sin. Guilt is declared by God on the basis of each person's particular nature.

There are indeed some who contend, that we are so lost through Adam's sin, as though we perished through no fault of our own, but only, because he had sinned for us. But Paul distinctly affirms, that sin extends to all who suffer its punishment: and this he afterwards more fully declares, when subsequently he assigns a reason why all the posterity of Adam are subject to the dominion of death; and it is even this—because we have all, he says, sinned. But to sin in this case, is to become corrupt and vicious; for the natural depravity which we bring, from our mother's womb, though it brings not forth immediately its own fruits, is yet sin before God, and deserves his vengeance: and this is that sin which they call original. For as Adam at his creation had received for us as well as for himself the gifts of God's favor, so by falling away from the Lord, he in himself corrupted, vitiated, depraved, and ruined our nature; for having been divested of God's likeness, he could not have generated seed but what was like himself. Hence we have all sinned; for we are all imbued with natural corruption, and so are become sinful and wicked.[24]

Notice the last clause here: the sin in which we all participate is that we are imbued with natural corruption. Furthermore, we are not guilty of Adam's particular sin, but he put us under a condition in which we are guilty when we individualize this corrupt nature. Randall Zachman reaches a similar conclusion in his analysis of Calvin's doctrine of sin. For Zachman, when Calvin asks, "how does Adam's sin become my sin simply by being born?" his answer is that "we have, therefore, all sinned, because we are imbued with natural corruption, and for this reason are wicked and perverse."[25] Whereas in later Reformed vocabulary, corruption is simply described as an inclination that does not render one culpable, Zachman correctly reads Calvin's nuance.[26]

---

24. John Calvin, *Commentary on the Epistle to the Romans* (Grand Rapids: Baker, 1997), Romans 5:12.

25. Randall C. Zachman, "John Calvin," *T&T Clark Companion to the Doctrine of Sin*, ed. Keith L. Johnson and David Lauber (Bloomsbury T&T Clark, 2016), 242.

26. Zachman still positions Calvin in the Federalist side of the equation. Ibid., 243.

One last problem with Allen's article: In Calvin's discussion of the assumption of a human nature by Christ,[27] Calvin contends that "Christ, by whom integrity was to be restored, was exempted from common *corruption*"[28] shutting at once the possibility to use original sin as an entryway into Christ's assumption of a fallen human nature. The virgin birth functions as the sanctifying point in which, although Christ would naturally assume a corrupted nature, the Holy Spirit hinders the natural course of nature. I argue that Calvin moves in this direction because in his doctrine of original sin, a corrupted nature would render Christ obnoxious to God and ultimately liable to punishment based on his particular concrete nature.

THE SANCTIFICATION OF CHRIST
IN CALVIN'S THEOLOGY

Calvin is known as the theologian of the Holy Spirit, but it is my contention in this section that his focus on the Spirit leads him to neglect the role of the Son in the act of assumption or union. Calvin's lack of treatment of the Son's role in the act of sanctification in the assumption implies a reversal of the Trinitarian order of action. In what follows, I will look to Calvin's treatment of the humanity of Christ in a few of his works and demonstrate that his notion of sanctification in Christ's human nature is solely restricted to the Holy Spirit.

Calvin starts his chapter "Christ Clothed in the Substance of Human Nature" by emphasizing that the humanity Christ took was one that came from the seed of Abraham and Jacob. Therefore, this seed cannot be created out of thin air, but is a real human body and soul (*contra* the Manichees and Marcionites).[29] The real humanity of Jesus is evidenced in Calvin's use of Hebrews 2:14: "Both he that sanctifieth and they who are sanctified are all of one: for which cause he is not ashamed to call them brethren." This sanctification is obviously connected to Christ's human nature and not his divinity, for the divine nature cannot be enriched in any way. Therefore, Calvin explains that in no other way could one say that Christ received the Spirit

---

27. Calvin, *Institutes* 2.13.1–4.
28. Ibid., 2.13.4. Emphasis added.
29. Calvin, *Institutes* 2.13.1.

for sanctification if it is not through his human nature. The argument is that sanctification or enrichment is here attributed to the Holy Spirit.[30]

The role of the Spirit is once again evidenced in his treatment of the virgin birth. According to Calvin, the Marcionites rejected the real humanity of Christ because they thought that Jesus would then be subjected to the common law that included all of the offspring of Adam—sin. Calvin answers this by stating that it is obvious from Scripture that Christ is righteous and without sin. The fact that he came from heaven (1 Cor 15:47) does not nullify his true humanity because he also came in the likeness of sinful flesh (Rom 8:3). Coming in the likeness of sinful flesh, however, does not mean that he is sinful because the Holy Spirit prevented sinfulness from coming in through Mary. Calvin contends, "We make Christ free of all stain not just because he was begotten of his mother without copulation with man, but because he was sanctified by the Spirit that the generation might be pure and undefiled as would have been true before Adam's fall."[31] Calvin asserts that the logic of Christ's unfallen nature is not due the fact that he does not have a human father since Mary could also have given him the corruption that came from Adam, but because of the work of the Spirit.[32]

Furthermore, the role of the Spirit, in effecting sanctification, is proved once more in *The Geneva Catechism*. The Catechism states,

Q52 M. You say that Christ behooved to become man, that he might, as it were, in our person accomplish the work of salvation?

S. So I think. For we must borrow of him whatever is wanting in ourselves: and this cannot be done in any other way.

---

30. Calvin, *Institutes* 2.13.1.

31. Calvin, *Institutes* 2.13.4.

32. This coheres with Kelly Kapic's conclusion in his article "The Son's Assumption of a Human Nature: A Call for Clarity," 154–66. Kapic asserts, "So how does Jesus escape this contamination and thus become able to act vicariously? The way Calvin maneuvers at this point is by turning to the importance of the sanctifying work of the Spirit. It is only 'because he was sanctified by the Spirit that the generation might be pure and undefiled as *would have been true before Adam's fall.*' He argues, accordingly, that when the scriptures refer to Jesus' purity or holiness it must be understood as a reference to his human nature, 'for it would have been superfluous to say that God is pure.' Since the original creation of humanity was good, sin is considered accidental rather than essential to human. Such purity of a true human nature after the fall is possible only by the Spirit's involvement, from conception to ascension. Therefore, reference to the virgin birth is primarily in order to stress both the true humanity of Christ and his 'incorruption in Adam's race,' rather than his divinity. In other words, there was never a time when his human nature was not sanctified by the Holy Spirit."

Q53 M. But why was that affected by the Holy Spirit, and not by the common and usual form of generation?

S. As the seed of man is entirely corrupt, it was necessary that the operation of the Holy Spirit should interfere in the generation of the Son of God, that he might not be affected by this contagion, but endued with the most perfect purity.[33]

Calvin's discussion of the assumption of human nature is completely focused on the Spirit's role in keeping the Son from corruption. No mention is made of the Son's assumption and work in sanctification. Note that the biblical language is that when Mary is elected to be the bearer of the savior, the Spirit came *upon her.* So says Luke 1:35, "And the angel answered her, "The Holy Spirit will *come upon you,* and the power of the Most High will overshadow *you;* therefore the child to be born will be called holy—the Son of God." Calvin, however, interprets such passages not only to mean that the mode of sanctification of Christ's human nature is through the Holy Spirit but also that it speaks to the unity of Christ's person. Calvin asserts:

This passage not only expresses a unity of person in Christ, but at the same time points out that, in clothing himself with human flesh, Christ is the Son of God. As the name, Son of God, belonged to the divine essence of Christ from the beginning, so now it is applied unitedly to both natures, because the secret and heavenly manner of generation has separated him from the ordinary rank of men. In other passages, indeed, with the view of asserting that he is truly man, he calls himself the Son of man (John 5:27); *but the truth of his human nature is not inconsistent with his deriving peculiar honor above all others from his divine generation, having been conceived out of the ordinary way of nature by the Holy Spirit.* This gives us good reason for growing confidence, that we may venture more freely to call God our Father, because his only Son, in order that we might have a Father in common with him, chose to be our brother.[34]

---

33. Calvin and Waterman, *The Catechism of the Church of Geneva* (Sydney, Australia: Wentworth Press, 2016), 15.

34. John Calvin's Commentaries: *Harmony of the Gospels* (Grand Rapids, Baker Books, 1974), Luke 1:35.

The argument here is commonly orthodox: the continuity with humanity is perceived in the flesh Christ receives from Mary. The discontinuity
is the vertical intersection of the Holy Spirit who interrupts the process
and creates discontinuity. Nonetheless, the honor received by Christ in his
human nature, being above all, is connected once again *only* to the Holy
Spirit's preservation.

Derek Thomas registers some dissatisfaction with Calvin's treatment
of the Holy Spirit as the agent of sanctification here:

> What was sanctified, and when? Was it the unfertilized ovum?
> Surely not. It makes little sense to speak of sanctifying a piece of
> tissue. Was it the fertilized ovum: the foetus itself? It seems impos-
> sible to speak of this being sanctified without implying that prior to
> such sanctification it was impure or sinful. ... It seems best to avoid
> altogether language which involves us in such difficulties. We need
> say no more than that the humanity of Christ was created by the
> Holy Spirit, rather than procreated by sexual intercourse, and that
> as such it partook of the essential character of all that God creates:
> it was very good.[35]

Even though Thomas does not see the necessity to speak of sanctification at all, his frustration is connected to the Holy Spirit's role in this process. For Thomas, one must speak merely of creation by God, not the Spirit's
sanctifying role in Christ's human nature. As I will show later, if one expos-
its the sanctification of Christ's human nature only through the Spirit, then
fallenness is still open (as Thomas correctly points out), because it becomes
overtly dependent on habitual grace. If the Son, as he creates, assumes and
sanctifies this nature, then there is no moment in which there is the need
of progressive sanctification toward moment—such progression is the
role of the Spirit. This is why the church has held to the *an-en-hypostasic*
tension: it both protects the incarnation from adoptionist tendencies and
correctly works with a person-nature distinction within the Trinity and the

---

35. Derek Thomas, "The Mediator of the Covenant" in *A Theological Guide to Calvin's
Institutes: Essays and Analysis* ed. David W. Hall and Peter A. Lillback (Phillipsburg, NJ: P&R
Publishing, 2015), 213.

Incarnation.[36] I fundamentally disagree with Derek Thomas's rejection of
the need of sanctification but suspect that his only category for this work
is one connected to habitual grace.

A few disclaimers: one must note that the discussion here is focused
on the Son's assumption of a human nature and not on the relationship of
the two natures and the person (on issues such as the *communicatio*). On
this latter subject, Calvin's treatment is anything but short.[37] This also is
not a discussion on the merits of the exaltation of Christ in Calvin's *corpus*.
Although the exaltation of Christ's human nature might have some relevance for the purposes of this article, the energy spent here is on trying to
find a mention of the Son's role in sanctifying his created human nature.[38]

---

36. The created human nature which the *Logos* assumed did not have a personalized
created human person (*an-hypostasis*), but it received its personalization *via* the assumption
of the person of the Son (*en-hypostasis*). Sanders says, "On the one hand, the human nature of
Jesus Christ is in fact a nature joined to a person, and therefore enhypostatic, or personalized.
But the person who personalizes the human nature of Christ is not a created human person
(like all the other persons personalizing the other human natures we encounter); rather it
is the eternal second person of the Trinity. So the human nature of Christ is personal, but
with a personhood from above. Considered in itself, on the other hand, and abstracted from
its personalizing by the eternal person of the Son, the human nature of Jesus Christ is simply
human nature, and is not personal. The human nature of Christ, therefore, is both anhypostatic (not personal in itself) and enhypostatic (personalized by union with the eternal person
of the Son)." See Scott Horrell et al., *Jesus in Trinitarian Perspective: An Intermediate Christology*,
ed. Fred Sanders and Klaus Issler (Nashville, TN: B&H Academic, 2007), 31.

Ignatius van Wyk compares Calvin and the Heildelberg Cathechism and asserts that in
contrast to the Hedielberg Catechism, Calvin omits the idea of the divine Son taking such
humanity and sanctifying, because Christ's divinity is presupposed: "In his First Catechism
of 1538, Calvin (in Hesselink 1997) says that these two phrases emphasise the humanness of
the Son of God. His divinity is presupposed and does not need further clarity." Furthermore,
he contends that Calvin was probably not fighting adoptionists in Geneva. That might help
explain why Calvin neglects the role of the Son in sanctifying his human nature. Ignatius
W. C. (Natie) van Wyk, " ' ... Conceived by the Holy Spirit and Born of the Virgin Mary': The
Exposition of the Heidelberg Catechism in the Light of Present-Day Criticism," *Hervormde
Teologiese Studies* 70, no. 1 (January 2014): 1–9. Muller offers another possible explanation:
"Calvin's thought focuses on the concrete Christ of history and the integrity of the *forma servi*
encountered by faith in the temporal dispensation of salvation." See Richard A. Muller, *Christ
and the Decree: Christology and Predestination in Reformed Theology from Calvin to Perkins* (Grand
Rapids: Baker Academic, 2008), 29.

37. See John Calvin, *Theological Treatises* (Philadelphia: Westminster Press, 1954);
Institutes 2.14.1. "Thus the Scriptures speak of Christ. See also Stephen Edmondson, *Calvin's
Christology* (Cambridge: Cambridge University Press, 2004), 216; Joseph N. Tylenda, "Calvin's
Understanding of the Communication of Properties," *WTJ* 38, no. 1 (September 1975): 54–65;
Stephen R. Holmes, "Reformed Varieties of the Communicatio Idiomatum," in *Person of Christ*
(London: T&T Clark, 2005), 70–86.

38. On the exaltation of Christ's human nature, see Robert Baylor, " 'With Him in Heavenly
Realms': Lombard and Calvin on Merit and the Exaltation of Christ," *IJST* 17, no. 2 (April 2015):

The debate over the exaltation of Christ's human nature in Calvin, relevant as it is, tends to focus on whether Christ was exalted by grace or by merit, but does not tap into the mode of impartation of this grace.[39]

Finally, some interpreters point to Calvin's treatment of the sacraments. It is true that when dealing with the Lord's Supper, Calvin talks about the Son giving life to flesh. Moreover, he states that the flesh of Christ "in its first condition it was subject to mortality; and now, endowed with immortality, it does not live through itself."[40] His discussion is not necessarily regarding how (by what mechanism) the flesh of Christ is imbued with life, but on the fact that it participates in the life of God, who has life in himself.[41]

REFORMED DEVELOPMENTS ON ORIGINAL SIN

Having noted that Calvin's theology of original sin was not one of strict immediate imputation of Adam's sin in his guilt, I will show that in the period known as Reformed Orthodoxy the theology of original sin developed into its form of double immediate imputation. The reason is polemic, exegetical, and theological and therefore demands dogmatic attention. It is through what is known as the "positive function of heresy" that Reformed theology responded to misconceptions. When error is raised and defended, orthodoxy needs to refine what has not yet been systematized.

Much of the attention given to the subject of the imputation of Adam's guilt is a fruit of the condemnation of Josué de la Place by the Synod of Charenton (1644-1645). Up until this point there was not enough clarity over the imputation of Adam's guilt (as seen in Calvin's exposition). Around 1640, Josué de la Place "defended a number of theses at the academy of

---

152-75; Alan W Gomes, "Faustus Socinus and John Calvin on the Merits of Christ," *Reformation & Renaissance Review* 12, no. 2/3 (August 2010): 189-205.

39. See Gomes, "Faustus Socinus and John Calvin on the Merits of Christ."

40. Calvin, *Institutes* 4.17.9.

41. J. Todd Billings, "United to God through Christ: Assessing Calvin on the Question of Deification," *Harvard Theological Review* 98, no. 3 (July 2005): 315-34. See also, J. Todd Billings, *Calvin, Participation, and the Gift: The Activity of Believers in Union with Christ* (New York: Oxford University Press, 2007), 134-37. Also see Julie Canlis, *Calvin's Ladder: A Spiritual Theology of Ascent and Ascension* (Grand Rapids: Eerdmans Pub. Co., 2010).

Saumur concerning the imputation of Adam's sin."[42] It is interesting to note that de la Place

> claimed Calvin's support for his own rejection of the representative notion advanced by his Reformed contemporaries. La Place recognized only a realistic relationship between Adam and humankind that served as the basis for the transmission of Adam's own corruption to his descendants. If individuals own any guilt as an aspect of original sin, he argued, it is guilt for the corruption residing in them by virtue of their natural descent from Adam. His doctrine admitted no place for the "immediate imputation" of guilt for Adam's actual transgression to humankind. La Place denied, moreover, the existence of any covenant between God and Adam—that notion that supplied a theoretical basis for the representative relationship recognized by his orthodox peers.[43]

Moreover, de la Place had other misconceptions, according to the Reformed, on the nature of imputation, such that he did not also believe in the imputation of Christ's active obedience.[44]

Herman Bavinck, an eclectic inheritor of Reformed Orthodox tradition, addressed the same errors of de la Place, but pointing to the New England theologian, Jonathan Edwards.[45] Due to Bavinck's clarity and eclecticism in his approach to theology, what follows tracks closely to his discussion on original sin. For Bavinck, Edwards fell into the same error as de la Place. Bavinck stated,

> [I]t is equally incorrect for us to draw from the fact that guilt and pollution always go together in sin the conclusion that the pollution is actually anterior to guilt. Jonathan Edwards in part arrived at this position because he tried to deduce the sinful deed from the

---

42. F. P. van Stam, *The Controversy over the Theology of Saumur, 1635–1650 : Disrupting Debates among the Huguenots in Complicated Circumstances* (Amsterdam: APA-Holland University Press, 1988), 179.

43. Aaron Clay Denlinger, "Calvin's Understanding of Adam's Relationship to His Posterity: Recent Assertions of the Reformer's 'federalism' Evaluated," *Calvin Theological Journal* 44, no. 2 (November 2009): 228.

44. Heber Carlos de Campos, *Doctrine in Development: Johannes Piscator and Debates over Christ's Active Obedience* (Grand Rapids: Reformation Heritage Books, 2017), 189.

45. On Bavinck's eclecticism, see Eglinton, *Trinity and Organism*.

sinful inclination that originated earlier and sought to explain the latter in terms of the natural principles inherent in humanity's lower nature. (J. Ridderbos, *Jonathan Edwards*, 171ff.) But this position was advocated decisively and candidly in the school of Saumur (France) by Placaeus [de la Place] and all the proponents of a mediate imputation of Adam's sin.[46]

Bavinck's rejection of mediate imputation *à la* de la Place and Edwards is inserted in his discussion of "Human Solidarity" and "Sin as Sin's Consequence." Paramount to Bavinck is that moral depravity does not arise later as a result of bad deeds, but it has a cause. The cause is Adam's originating sin, but this does make God an arbitrary tyrant that holds people guilty by sheer force of will.[47]

To understand Bavinck's response to the charge of arbitrariness, one must understand his organic motif.[48] He claims that "humanity is not an aggregate of individuals, but an organic unity, one race, one family."[49] Nathaniel Gray Sutanto explains that by "organic," Bavinck means "An archetypal unity-in-diversity in the Godhead implies that creation displays an ectypal unity-in-diversity"[50] So, a mere realist account of the transmission of sin cannot account for this ectype in an appropriate manner. For Bavinck, a realist account of transmission of sin treats Adam as a private person and cannot escape the charge of arbitrariness.[51] Only when one sees unity-in-diversity as federal, instead of physically, one can make sense of the transmission of sin without falling into pure voluntarism.[52]

The genius of Bavinck in this section is to see that if "Adam's trespass had been ours in the realistic sense, we would also be responsible for all the other sins of Adam, all the sins of Eve, even the sins of our ancestors,

---

46. *RD* III, 109.

47. *RD* III, 101.

48. For a detailed explanation to Bavinck's Organic motif related to original sin, see Nathaniel Sutanto, "Herman Bavinck on the Image of God and Original Sin," *IJST* 18, no. 2 (April 2016): 174–90.

49. *RD* III, 102.

50. Sutanto, "Herman Bavinck on the Image of God and Original Sin," 174.

51. *RD* III, 102.

52. *RD* III, 102.

for we were included in them."[53] Necessarily if the only manner of transmission was physical, then it would be hard to see how Christ could escape
from original sin itself.[54]

   This realist, which Bavinck also calls mediative, account of transmission of sin would not only render Jesus as fallen, but also lead to a certain
kind of universalism in the parallel between Adam and Christ. For if Adam
is only physically representative of all, then Jesus follows the same pattern
and represents all the men. Bavinck illustrates the organic bond as federal
representational by suggesting that moral unity is stronger than physical
unity. For example, fathers, mothers, teachers and tutors have "greatest
influence on those under their jurisdiction. Their life and conduct decides
the fortunes of their subordinates."[55] Hence, Christ stands as a representative of those united to him in the same representational manner that Adam
stands, not mere physical but as their moral, rational, and spiritual head.

   Next, Bavinck reflects on the interconnectedness of pollution and guilt.
He does that by appealing to a certain psychological analysis of the fall.
It was not the act of eating the fruit by itself that brought the fall into
world, but reflecting on James 1:15 Bavinck states that the eating of the
fruit was the "first fully matured sin."[56] He affirms that before, during,
and after eating the forbidden fruit, humankind's relation to God was
already changed. And as such, "they did not first become one thing and
then another."[57] Bavinck means here that they did not become impure
or corrupted and only after some particular act they became guilty. The
change happened when Adam "progressively detached himself further
from God and his law."[58]

   According to Bavinck, here lies the error of the mediative view held by
Jonathan Edwards. For Edwards, guilt is posterior to pollution. Edwards'
artifice for his argumentation is that he "tried to deduce a sinful deed from
the sinful inclination that it originated earlier and sought to explain the

---

53. *RD* III, 103.
54. *RD* III, 103.
55. *RD* III, 104.
56. *RD* III, 108.
57. *RD* III, 108.
58. *RD* III, 108.

latter in terms of natural principles inherent in humanity's lower nature."[59] Moreover, the New England theologian created a distinction between natural and moral impotence to defend that fallen humankind has a "natural, but not the moral power to do good."[60] Bavinck views this line of argument as leading to a denial of total depravity. For Bavinck, the entire human person has fallen and therefore the Reformed correctly spoke of "natural impotence."[61] By this, the Dutch theologian means that the inability to do good is congenital and not introduced by environment or custom.

Bavinck ties the Edwardsean position back to the school of Saumur (de la Place's school), and explains why this view is objectionable. There must be an antecedent judgement ($\kappa\rho\iota\mu\alpha$) and this judgement on one human has as its content the sentence ($\kappa\alpha\tau\alpha\kappa\rho\iota\mu\alpha$) upon all his progeny because "being born in this state of guilt, impure, and depravity is the execution of the sentence passed by God on Adam's trespass."[62] Moreover, Sutanto has provided a fine analysis of how the federal position laid out by Bavinck, coupled with his organic motif, evades the charge of arbitrariness or even the charge of legal fiction.[63] Sutanto states,

A response to this worry is inherent within Bavinck's account of anthropology. If the imago Dei does not merely consider individual human beings, but the entirety of the human race as an organic unity, the objection that one could not be held responsible for the sins of another loses its force. That is, for the objection to exert pressure, one would need to bear the burden of proof to provide a theological rationale concerning why the entire human race should not be considered as a single organic whole, or why the imago Dei should only have its referent in human individuals, and not the entire human race. Considered this way, ethical solidarity with the federal head is not to render oneself vulnerable to

---

59. *RD* III, 109.

60. *RD* III, 121.

61. *RD* III, 122.

62. *RD* III, 110.

63. For a recent discussion of the charges of arbitrariness and legal fiction, see Oliver Crisp, "Original Sin," in *Christian Dogmatics: Reformed Theology for the Church Catholic*, ed. Michael Allen and Scott R. Swain (Grand Rapids: Baker Academic, 2016), 202–5.

some "legal fiction." Rather, this federal make-up is precisely that
which respects the triune and relational shape of those who bear
God's image.[64]

Sutanto, who also refers to Crisp's worries, remembers that Bavinck is
not placing the federal headship of Adam or Christ on a mere voluntarist
(from divine will alone) or even intellectualist (stemming from God acting
according to his character) fashion. God did not just choose Adam to be
humanity's representative and arbitrarily placed Adam's guilt on his progeny. Rather, the makeup of created reality is one that has within itself a
pattern of unity-in-diversity that is ectypal. Because transmission of sin is
not physical, then Christ is able to be in solidarity with humankind without
actually partaking of the sin that takes hold of humankind.

EXCURSUS ON ROMANS 5:12–21

The central idea in this text is the juxtaposition of two men. One who dis-
obeyed God and another who obeyed. According to Schreiner, the whole
section is building up from the theme of hope that Paul laid out on verse
1–11 from chapter 5. For Schreiner, "Christ has overturned the negative consequences of Adam's sin. The power of grace is stronger than sin and death,
and thus believers can be assured that they will reign in life (verse17) and
that grace will reign and result in eternal life (verse 21)."[65] Having framed
the discussion with the victory of grace one needs to deal with the difficulty
of verse 12. (Διὰ τοῦτο ὥσπερ δι' ἑνὸς ἀνθρώπου ἡ ἁμαρτία εἰς τὸν κόσμον
εἰσῆλθεν καὶ διὰ τῆς ἁμαρτίας ὁ θάνατος, καὶ οὕτως εἰς πάντας ἀνθρώπους
ὁ θάνατος διῆλθεν ἐφ' ᾧ πάντες ἥμαρτον.)

The inherent and well noted difficulty for the current discussion lies
on how to translate ἐφ' ᾧ. The linguistic construction can have several
meanings and it depends highly upon the context. Schreiner points out
that instead of focusing on what is the technical linguistic referent of ἐφ'
ᾧ one should see the broader referent of the idea of ἐφ' ᾧ.[66] In this case, it
seems that θάνατος is the referent because Paul is painting a larger parallel

---

64. Sutanto, "Herman Bavinck on the Image of God and Original Sin," 190.

65. Thomas R. Schreiner, *Romans,* Baker Exegetical Commentary on the New Testament
(Grand Rapids: Baker Academic, 1998), 271.

66. Ibid., 264.

between Christ and Adam. While Christ brings life, Adam brings (διῆλθεν) death. Once the referent has been discovered, it is still unclear on how to translate the ἐφ' ᾧ construction.

Moo has pointed out that the structure of the verse fits neatly into a chiastic structure that should read as follows:

A sin (12a) produces
B death (12b)
B all die (12c)
A because all sin (12d)[67]

As such, the ἐφ' ᾧ conjunctional structure would render a causal meaning. Moo bases this on the fact that the chiastic structure of verse 12 renders sin both as the manner to which death came into the world, but also the fact that all die is tied to sin as well. Therein a translation that reads "on the account of (ἐφ' ᾧ) his death, all sinned" is possible.

Moo rejects the mediative view based on the fact that it cannot account for verses 15–18 appropriately (γὰρ τῷ τοῦ ἑνὸς παραπτώματι οἱ πολλοὶ ἀπέθανον; τὸ μὲν γὰρ κρίμα ἐξ ἑνὸς εἰς κατάκριμα; γὰρ τῷ τοῦ ἑνὸς παραπτώματι ὁ θάνατος ἐβασίλευσεν). A reading such as "because of one man's trespass many became corrupted in the human nature and therefore sinned," is unlikely to do justice to these verses. Hence, Moo concludes that all sinned must have some corporate meaning. " 'Sinning' not as a voluntary act of sin in 'one's own person,' but sinning 'in and with' Adam."[68]

Moreover, Francis Turretin gives a few reasons why the ἐφ' ᾧ structure must be translated as causative. First, because the apostle carefully states through the passage that death passed to everyone not as if personally everyone has sinned in themselves. Second, the parallel between Adam and Christ is "in the thing, but not in the mode of the thing." Meaning that while Adam brought guilt and condemnation, Christ brought grace and justification. Third, the treatment of the actual sin of Adam and the necessary guilt fits better with an account of justification. Those who are justified are justified of guilt.

---

67. Douglas J. Moo, *The Epistle to the Romans*, The New International Commentary on the New Testament (Grand Rapids: Eerdmans, 1996), 321.

68. Moo, *The Epistle to the Romans*, 326.

Henri Blocher has posed a recent mediative treatment of this passage. Blocher seems to have a view similar to what I described as Calvin's. He asserts,

> How did punishment, death, reach all persons on the basis of (*eph' ho*) their actual sinning? It reached them in the same way that death entered Adam's person: since we are all in Adam, the head, sin could be reckoned to them according to the terms of the Adamic covenant, as offshoots of his sin. This is manifest in the imputation possible independently of Adam. [Blocher continues] The hypothesis I propose easily accounts for the imperfect symmetry between the two heads of humankind. Adam's role is more firmly cast than in the 'looser' reading of Romans 5; at the same time, the unattested and difficult thesis of the imputation of an *alien* sin is avoided— without downplaying the tragic realism of the Augustinian human predicament.[69]

In summary, Blocher wants to avoid the two tendencies of either tightening or loosening the relationship of Adam and his offspring. *Prima facie*, it seems like there is a psychological appeal for this position since no one wants to be guilty of another's sin. Schreiner, however, has argued, in conversation with Blocher, that Blocher's arguments fails on at least two levels.

> First, his claim that the sin of human beings mirror Adam's sin veers away from what Paul actually teaches in Romans 5:12–19, for Paul specifically and emphatically distinguishes the sin of those who live in the era between Adam and Moses from Adam's sin. Second, the text does not share Blocher's squeamishness about alien guilt, for it teaches that human beings are sinners and condemned (and hence guilty!) because of Adam's one sin. Just as human beings are righteous because of what Christ has done, so too they are guilty because of what Adam has done.[70]

---

69. Henri Blocher, *Original Sin: Illuminating the Riddle* (Downers Grove, IL: IVP Academic, 1602), 77, 80.

70. Thomas Schreiner, "Original sin and Original Death: Romans 5:12–19" in *Adam, the Fall, and Original Sin: Theological, Biblical, and Scientific Perspectives*, ed. Hans Madueme and Michael Reeves. (Grand Rapids: Baker Academic, 2014), 277.

Adam's sin has a federal *and* typological character. It is federal because his sin passed through others *via* the unity-in-diversity relationship he has with other men and women. His sin is not isolated and private but it is passed through succeeding generations by God's accounting of that unity-in-diversity relationship. Is also typological because humans also sin. They sin after the pattern of the sin of Adam. It should not be an "either/or" because the exegetical moves from Paul grant both representation and responsibility. As Schreiner aptly notes, "the forensic cannot be separated from what is actual. Those who are constituted as sinners in Adam become sinners in practice, and those who are counted righteous in Christ live righteously."[71]

ORIGINAL SIN AND THE FALLEN CHRIST

The exposition above on propagation of sin should frame the discussion of Christ's assumption of human nature in dialogue with Karl Barth and Thomas Torrance. Original sin in the Reformed tradition after Calvin was established as a tale of two federal heads—Adam and Christ. If the above sketch is true to the biblical data, then Christ and Adam both stand in the covenant of works. They are both sons of God whose humanity is determinative for their representatives. Both Barth and Torrance have some unique contributions to the doctrine of original sin and shall, again, be evaluated according to the exposition above.

KARL BARTH

The affirmation of Christ and Adam as representative of humanity is clear in Barth's works.[72] As shown before, Christ does not adapt to Adam, but Christ, being the true image *is* the real man. One of the ways that Barth makes this point is by asserting that our existence in Adam does not have an independent status. He means that Christ is the only one able to stand as true representative for humankind. Again, our union with Adam is less essential than our union with Christ exactly because of the way in which God organized things. In Christ, the relationship between the one and the many is a gracious relationship.

---

71. Thomas Schreiner, "Original sin and Original Death," 286.
72. *CD* IV/1, 501.

Regarding the transmission of sin, Barth forcefully rejects hereditary sin and even realist accounts as "hopelessly naturalistic, deterministic, and even fatalistic," but he still wants to keep the term original sin (*Ursünde*). He reasons that original sin still keeps the "voluntary and responsible life of every man."[73] Embedded in this affirmation is Barth's rejection of the Reformation doctrine of total depravity. For as, Shao Kai Tseng reminds us, "Barth is emphatic that the good nature of human beings remains in the fallen sinner despite the total destruction of the imago."[74] Much of this reformulation of the doctrine of original sin resides in Barth's restructuring of the image of God as Jesus Christ himself. As Tseng reminds us again, "he [Barth] would come to redefine imago Dei as none other than Jesus Christ himself, who as the very relationship between God and humanity is a 'copy' of the triune relationship that is the "divine original" (this is the crux of Barth's famous *analogia relationis*)."[75]

Hence, goodness is ascribed to humankind because humankind is made in the pattern of Christ. And Christ's determination to be *for us* has also brought a determination for an identification with us in our fall. Of course, as pointed out in chapter 2, this does not mean that God has sin in himself (*ad intra*), but simply that solidarity goes back as far as it can.

The move of representation here is justified in that we are dealing with "two great contexts, or unities, in which all men stand."[76] Adam belongs only to the past and has no future.[77] His verdict is only seen in the final day through Jesus Christ. Christ embraces Adam prospectively in election and as Christ comes into the far country.

The combination of Barth's rejection of any hereditary sin, with his modified representational theology through actualism and election, leads to Christ's assumption of a fallen nature within a matrix that is not self-contradictory. When Adam's representation is weakened in order to make his classical, Christocentric move, Barth must place sin somewhere

---

73. CD IV/1, 501.

74. Shao Kai Tseng, " 'Non Potest Non Peccare': Karl Barth on Original Sin and the Bondage of the Will," *Neue Zeitschrift für Systematicsche Theologie und Religionsphilosophie* 60, no. 2 (2018): 199.

75. Tseng, "Non Potest Non Peccare," 200.

76. CD IV/1, 501.

77. Ibid., 502.

in its relationship to God. After all, Barth knows that theology is about God and all things in relation to God. Christ's flesh, then, bears the full weight of sin in his relationship to God in this far country. Exactly because Christ does not "wait" for Adam but proactively is *for us*, sin's location is able to shift freely. Moreover, the fact that sin does not belong to this existence but is an impossible possibility makes sin something that can never determine reality as it is. As Webster asserts:

> One important consequence is that Barth is led to speak of sin as
> "an impossible possibility" (III/2, page 146)—if to be human is to
> be united to Christ, then sin cannot be definitive of human being.
> Barth's point is not that sin is not a real fact of our existence; it is
> that sin is a contradiction of the very constitution of human being.
> To decide for sin is not to decide for a possibility which, however
> dreadful it may be, is equally as real an actualization of human
> being as the life of obedience to God. To decide for sin is to negate
> what one inescapably is as a human being, and therefore to adopt an
> impossibility as if it were merely one more way of being a creature.[78]

Therefore, the question of responsibility, guilt, and pollution are less relevant than what it was for the Post-Reformation. Given that neither Barth nor Torrance (or anyone surveyed for this work for that matter) affirmed that Christ actively sinned, but that only that his flesh or human nature was tainted by sin, *prima facie*, Barth's theology of sin escapes the charge of pollution entailing guilt.

Nonetheless, the articulation of sin as impossible possibility, with pastoral solidarity, and actualism must account for the coherence of the biblical testimony in exegesis. Theological logic does not guarantee biblical fidelity. Theology must preserve the judgements of Scripture even when it uses different concepts. Romans 5 is a key text on how to articulate the relationship of Christ, Adam, and sin. It does not mean, however, that Barth had no interest in the exegetical movements of Romans 5, but because he views Adam's representation through Christ then he is committed to read the passage in a certain way. Creative reality (Adam, obviously, included) provides the external basis of the covenant of grace. Barth states:

---

78. J. B Webster, *Barth* (New York: Continuum, 2000), 102.

The covenant whose history had still to commence was the covenant which, as the goal appointed for creation and the creature, made creation necessary and possible, and determined and limited the creature. If creation was the external basis of the covenant, the latter was the internal basis of the former. If creation was the formal presupposition of the covenant, the latter was the material presupposition of the former. If creation takes precedence historically, the covenant does so in substance. If the proclamation and foundation of the covenant is the beginning of the history which commences after creation, the history of creation already contains, as the history of the being of all creatures, all the elements which will subsequently meet and be unified in this event and the whole series of events which follow; in the history of Israel, and finally and supremely in the history of the incarnation of the Son of God.[79]

Therefore, it is inappropriate to speak of Adam's precedence or equal representation because the covenant is only present in Christ's gracious election. "For there is re vera only one covenant, as there is only one God. The fact that Cocceius and his followers could not and would not say that, is what one should not follow them in, not in the older form, and even less in the modern form."[80] The dangers of covenant theology as explored in the above exposition of Romans 5:12 is that it leads to a historicism of grace or even Pelagianism according to Barth.[81]

These commitments of Barth, though they can make sense of Christ's assumption of fallen flesh regarding original sin, hardly explain the order of creation. As in previous chapters, the order of revelation cannot contradict ordering *ad intra*. The typological move "Adam then Christ" presupposes that Christ comes in created reality and becomes a man. Although it is true that Christ tells us what it really means to be human, his humanity is derived in creation. Taking its cues from a fear of abstraction, Barth's movement asserts that we can only know God and the things of God from

---

79. CD III/1, 231–32.

80. Rinse Herman Reeling Brouwer, "Karl Barth's Encounter with the Federal Theology of Johannes Cocceius: Prejudices, Criticisms, Outcomes and Open Questions," *Zeitschrift für Dialektische Theologie.* Supp. Series 4 (2010): 167.

81. See also, Cornelis P Venema, "Recent Criticisms of the 'covenant of Works' in the Westminster Confession of Faith," *Mid-America Journal of Theology* 9, no. 2 (1993): 165–98.

what has been revealed in the work of Christ. Two "mega-doctrines" direct the way for this movement: Trinity and Christology. Sanders, however, notes that work of John Webster reverted attention to two distributive doctrines that tend to correct the emphasis given in this movement: Trinity and creation. Without a proper doctrine of creation to refer to God's saving action, "the existence and history of created things may be assumed as given, quasi-necessary."[82]

In conclusion, once Barth establishes creation as the external context of the covenant, then Adam's place is less significant for the location of original sin. Christ's human nature easily absorbs sin in a history that reflects God's movement of condescension. The problem with this movement is that, as Webster said,

> The Christian doctrine of creation treats three principal topics: the identity of the creator, the divine act of creating and the several natures and ends of created things. These topics are materially ordered: teaching about the identity of the creator governs what is said about his creative act and about what he creates. In early Christian developments of the doctrine of creation out of nothing, much turned on the perception that God's radical perfection requires extensive revisions both of how the act of creation is to be understood (it can have no material cause) and of the natures of the beings created by this act. Of course, the order of inquiry does not necessarily conform to the material order: reflection on the doctrine of creation may take its rise with any one of the topics. But reflection will not reach its term.[83]

Once one subsumes created reality into whatever form of Christology, then Redemption is somehow prior to creation. This artifice however, as shown by Webster entails a form of identity that is incoherent with the order in God himself.[84]

---

82. Fred Sanders in "These Three Atone: Trinity and Atonement," in *T&T Clark Companion to Atonement* ed. Adam J. Johnson (New York: Bloomsbury T&T Clark, 2017), 26.

83. John Webster, " 'Love Is Also a Lover of Life': Creatio Ex Nihilo and Creaturely Goodness," *Mod. Theol.* 29, no. 2 (April 1, 2013): 157.

84. See Richard A. Muller, "A Note on 'christocentrism' and the Imprudent Use of Such Terminology," WTJ 68, no. 2 (2006): 253–60.

T. F. TORRANCE

The danger of externality is once again brought to the fore in Torrance's theology of original sin. From the very start, he is critical that federal theology has opted for a contractual view of God's relationship to the world. Torrance fears that the *homoousion* principle is damaged once one treats the relationship of God and the world (Adam in this case) as a set of preconditions.

The *homoousion* principle is not necessarily related to God and the world being of one and the same nature. It is, however, related to our knowledge of God and his relationship to us in the fact that it cannot be of a different order. Taking his cues from Karl Barth himself, Torrance claims that our knowledge is kataphysical, instead of mainly metaphysical. Just as in science, Albert Einstein proposed a certain revolution in how we come to understand things only as they relate to each other and to us; theology has a scientific approach by letting the object of study determine the method. So, our knowledge of God is according (*kata*) to what God chooses to reveal to us and our receptivity to that revelation.[85]

Federal theology, according to the Torrances, "distorts the nature of the Father, presenting Him primarily as a Judge and Lawgiver and only a Father to those who satisfy the requirements of the Law."[86] It is a theology that distances itself from true knowledge of God as Father and our relationship as sons and daughters to favor a certain dualistic relationship of law and obedience. "Federal Calvinism presents a covenant of works for all and a covenant of grace only for the elect. This means that God is related to all of humanity in terms of law, but only to some in terms of grace."[87] For Torrance, to treat the relationship of God and Adam as legal

---

85. I owe this summary to Kevin Vanhoozer, "T. F. Torrance's Kataphysical Poetics: How the Incarnation Relates Science to Theology | Henry Center," Henry Center for Theological Understanding (blog), February 2, 2018, http://henrycenter.tiu.edu/resource/t-f-torrances-kataphysical-poetics-how-the-incarnation-relates-science-to-theology/.

86. Alexandra Sophie Radcliff, "The Claim of Humanity in Christ: Salvation and Sanctification in the Theology of T. F. and J.B. Torrance" (PhD Thesis, University of St Andrews, 2014), 24.

87. Radcliff, "The Claim of Humanity in Christ," See also a more critical description of another Torrance, J. B. Torrance's idea of covenant of works in Venema, "Recent Criticisms of the 'covenant of Works' in the Westminster Confession of Faith," 174.

means that God acts with creation in abstract terms "as though it were the acting out of a plan."[88]

Also taking cues from McLeod Campbell, Torrance insists that the sonship of Christ must be understood in perfect harmony with the law, because the law is the expression of God's love as is also the Son. As Torrance said, "God's law is God's own heart '*come out in the shape of a law*'. It is the law of Love."[89] This move is what has been known in Torrance as the preference of the *filial* over the *legal* approach.[90] By preferring filial language, Torrance is able to assert that the atonement is better understood as essentially moral, spiritual, and physical.[91] Only a propitiatory movement that takes place within the "mediatorial Person and obedient Life of Christ from his birth ... to his death and resurrection" is able to avoid transactional and external views of the atonement. Because the atonement is not an external reality, the Son bears in his life the "wrath of God and his righteous judgement against sin."[92] And he does so even physically because Christ rendered this "expiatory confession ... in our name."[93]

One problem with Torrance's filial over federal schema is that it has to first account for the exegesis of Romans 5. A second problem is that you still have to deal with the totality of human nature. The way that Torrance talks about Adam, Jesus, and humanity in its "kataphysical poetics" rejects the causal and logical relation between God and the world. According to Torrance, this is due to a dependence on Aristotelian metaphysics that sees a ready reference between God and the world as a movement from down to up. For Torrance, human nature correctly has to be identified with Jesus Christ.

---

88. Thomas F. Torrance, *Scottish Theology: From John Knox to John McLeod Campbell* (Edinburgh: Bloomsbury T&T Clark, 2000), 292.

89. Ibid., 298.

90. Ibid.

91. Ibid.

92. Ibid., 299.

93. Ibid.

CONCLUDING THOUGHTS ON ORIGINAL
SIN AND THE *NON-ASSUMPTUS*

Despite being the only part of Christian theology that can be empirically proven, the issue of original sin continues to be debated. Plain observation all around confirms the reality of sin. The manner of transmission invokes even more heated debate because it summons to the conversation the problem of responsibility.

By resourcing Herman Bavinck, in this chapter I aimed to use his organic motif in order to first, avoid the charge of arbitrariness on how sin is transmitted. And second, to demonstrate how the unity-in-distinction provides a good *theolegoumena* in order to speak of Jesus's solidarity with humankind and avoid the assumption of sin. Jesus's solidarity with us bespeaks the essential features of what constitutes human nature without actually resorting to sin as part of that. By refuting realistic impulses that conflate transmission of sin with physical procreation, Bavinck is able to indirectly provide a language that avoids the pitfalls of complete solidarity that entails the assumption of sin. Nonetheless, at the same time he was able to speak of a complete humanity in the savior.

Karl Barth and Thomas Torrance's rejection of federalism puts them at a compromising position on how to ascribe to Jesus and Adam any kind of meaningful representation. By diminishing this representation of Adam they are unable to keep the coherence of created reality: that the Son comes in the context of creation to restore humankind from the guilt of Adam.

7

CONCLUSION

The thesis of this work is that those who argue for the Son's assumption of a fallen human nature are mistaken because they either work with a faulty notion of the nature of the hypostatic union, or invert Trinitarian order, or work with a defective notion of original sin. In order to prove these mistakes, I set out in each chapter to provide a positive way to talk about the incarnation. Each chapter contributes by creating a theological fence, so to speak, on how to talk about the act of assumption.

It is not my intention to charge anyone with heresy. Both Barth and Torrance strove to speak about the Son with the greatest respect, even as they were engaged in revision of Christian tradition. Moreover, both Barth and Torrance affirm the Nicene-Constantinople formulation. The major differences happen on the implications of the Trinitarian action once you have a different metaphysical framework. So, for example, when Barth reworks God's activity in actualistic fashion, we have to take Barth at his own words and scheme. And even though at times we compare Barth with Thomas Aquinas, or Torrance with the Post-Reformed, these comparisons serve only the purpose to evaluate the coherence of their own methods. I am not necessarily comparing something very foreign to Barth or Torrance. Barth's actualism has to make sense of Trinitarian action somehow.

So, when discussing the inseparable operations of the Trinity, first one has to make sense of how the church has historically made sense of this activity as it relates to the incarnation. It is not three happenings, but one, or that an act to be properly construed has both passivity and activity embedded in it. When Barth's theology is evaluated on its own terms it has also to account for one happening or some sort of inseparable action. His theology seems to fail when the determination of the human essence assumed by the Son is the Godhead who surrounds this man like a garment (something external to the condition of this man).[1] This position yields a rejection of any *inward* disposition of the Son caused by himself or it also fails to account for a theology of missions, but as I said before, if we follow Thomas' concepts of invisible missions as a corollary of the *opera trinitatis ad extra sunt indivisa*, then the *inward* disposition of the Son is breathed out from himself with the Spirit yielding a certain disposition and state of blessing. This is because the Spirit is sent by the Son into himself and that invisible mission is consistent with the work of the Spirit—who comes as the perfecter and finisher of something started by the Father and the Son.

The chapter on grace of union and habitual grace follows the chapter on inseparable operations clarifying some of its key insights. The use of habitual grace supplements the theology of inner dispositions as a corollary of the divine mission of the Holy Spirit and the *an-en-hypostatic* distinction. Retrieving Thomas Aquinas, I showed that "the mission of the Son is prior, in the order of nature, to the mission of the Holy Spirit, even as in the order of nature the Holy Spirit proceeds from the Son, and love from wisdom."[2] Hence, the grace of personal union precedes habitual grace because God's actions in time cannot contradict his life *ad intra*. With this in mind I engaged the fallen Christ proposal and demonstrated that Barth and Torrance worked with some measure of growth in grace and sanctification that ultimately would render the personal union viable. In doing that, even if unwillingly, they have logically placed some sort of habitual grace in front of personal grace.

The discussion on the doctrine of original sin aimed to build another way in which one can talk about the human nature of Christ vis-à-vis sin. A Post-Reformed doctrine of original sin, especially seen through the lens of Herman Bavinck, provides a unity-in-distinction manner in which we can talk about Jesus' relation to human nature in general. Jesus is representative of humankind, insofar they are ingrafted in him through faith, but he is not physically united to humankind *as if he has* to inherit the same mistakes of Adam or his progenitors. Following a purely realistic, mediative view of the transmission of sin would only render that one would be responsible and actually guilty for the sins of all his previous generations.

---

1. *CD* IV/1, 94.
2. *ST* III. Q7. A13. co.

These dogmatic reflections served as a humble way to provide the church with a certain apparatus to think about the humanity of Christ and his relationship to sin. Even though through the course of the book a polemical note struck some force, it is with the hope that the *loci* of Trinity, Christology, sin, and sanctification might better interact with each other that this work was written. It is only when we give up doing systematic theology on a blank sheet of paper in which each *locus* receives some proof-texts that we can move beyond the "he said, she said" theological debates. Although Barth receives his fair share of critiques in this work, I can still remember one cannot but be awe-struck by how he brought every *loci* to bear on another. There were simply no isolated *loci* as also there is no independent discipline. As C. Kavin Rowe states,

> [T]he kind of unity in interpretive practice upon which we want to insist is not a unity of two independent tasks, as if in good Gablerian fashion biblical scholars could simply hand their descriptive work over to the systematic theologians for contemporary construction, thereby "linking" the two separate projects together. Rather, the unity envisaged here operates at a much deeper level in that it calls for a subtle permeation or interpenetration of exegesis and dogmatics in the act of interpretation. In this way—to take two examples from my own ecclesial tradition—the unity of the interpretive enterprise is akin to what one senses in the prefaces to Calvin's *Institutes of the Christian Religion* (ICR) or in the programmatic criticisms expressed over three centuries later in Adolf Schlatter's brilliant essay "The Theology of the New Testament and Dogmatics"[...] dogmatics is something primary (*ein Erstes*) which influences all our looking back to what has happened.[3]

Dogmatics is primary but never isolated, because it furnishes the language that the church needs to speak properly about the Trinity, Christ, sin, and sanctification.

The concepts retrieved and developed here are in the service of the church vis-à-vis the rising of recent challenges to Christ's human nature.

---

3. Christopher Kavin Rowe, "For Future Generations: Worshipping Jesus and the Integration of the Theological Disciplines," *Pro Ecclesia* 17, no. 2 (2008): 205.

As stated before, this is not necessarily a battle of heresy vs. orthodoxy, but an attempt to provide the church with a better and more sophisticated vocabulary to talk about the incarnation.

BIBLIOGRAPHY

—

Adams, Marilyn McCord. *What Sort of Human Nature? Medieval Philosophy and the Systematics of Christology*. Milwaukee: Marquette University Press, 1999.

Ahn, Ho-Jin. "The Humanity of Christ: John Calvin's Understanding of Christ's Vicarious Humanity." *Scottish Journal of Theology* 65, no. 2 (2012): 145–58.

Allen, David L. *Hebrews*. New American Commentary. Nashville, TN: B&H, 2010.

Allen, Pauline, and Brownen Neil, eds. *The Oxford Handbook of Maximus the Confessor*. New York: Oxford University Press, 2015.

Allen, R. Michael. "Calvin's Christ: A Dogmatic Matrix for Discussion of Christ's Human Nature." *International Journal of Systematic Theology* 9, no. 4 (October 2007): 382–97.

———. *The Christ's Faith: A Dogmatic Account*. New York: Bloomsbury T&T Clark, 2009.

———. *Sanctification*. New Studies in Dogmatics, edited by Scott R. Swain. Grand Rapids: Zondervan, 2017.

Allen, R. Michael, and Scott R. Swain, eds. *Christian Dogmatics: Reformed Theology for the Church Catholic*. Grand Rapids: Baker Academic, 2016.

Anatolios, Khaled, and Brian Daley. *Retrieving Nicaea: The Development and Meaning of Trinitarian Doctrine*. Grand Rapids: Baker Academic, 2011.

Aquinas, Thomas. *Summa Contra Gentiles*. Turnhout, Belgium: Brepols, 2010.

———. *Summa Theologiae: Complete Set*. Edited by The Aquinas Institute. Lander, WY: The Aquinas Institute, 2012.

Arcadi, James M. "Kryptic or Cryptic? The Divine Preconscious Model of the Incarnation as a Concrete-Nature Christology." *Neue Zeitschrift für Systematische Theologie und Religionsphilosophie* 58, no. 2 (2016): 229–43.

Augustine. "On the Trinity." Translated Arthur West Haddan,. *A Select Library of the Nicene and Post-Nicene Fathers*, edited by Philip Schaff, 3:17–228. 1886. Reprint, Grand Rapids: Eerdmans, 1978.

———. *Sermons 51–94*. Translated by Edmund Hill. Brooklyn, NY: New City Press, 1992.

Ayres, Lewis. *Augustine and the Trinity*. Cambridge: Cambridge University Press, 2014.

———. *Nicaea and Its Legacy: An Approach to Fourth-Century Trinitarian Theology*. Oxford: Oxford University Press, 2004.

Balthasar, Hans Urs von. *Cosmic Liturgy: The Universe According to Maximus the Confessor*. 3rd ed. San Francisco: Ignatius Press, 2003.

Barth, Karl. *Christ and Adam: Man and Humanity in Romans 5*. Eugene, OR: Wipf & Stock, 2004.

———. *Church Dogmatics*. 4 vols. Edinburgh: T&T Clark, 1956–1975.

Bauerschmidt, Frederick Christian, and Thomas Aquinas. *Holy Teaching: Introducing the Summa Theologiae of St. Thomas Aquinas*. Grand Rapids: Brazos Press, 2005.

Bavinck, Herman. *Reformed Dogmatics*. 4 vols. Edited by John Bolt. Translasted by John Vriend. Grand Rapids: Baker Academic, 2006.

Baylor, Robert. " 'With Him in Heavenly Realms': Lombard and Calvin on Merit and the Exaltation of Christ." *International Journal of Systematic Theology* 17, no. 2 (April 2015): 152–75.

Beeke, Joel R. *Assurance of Faith*. 2nd ed. New York: Peter Lang, 1994.

Beeke, Joel R., and Mark Jones. *A Puritan Theology: Doctrine for Life*. Grand Rapids: Reformation Heritage Books, 2012.

Belt, Henk Van Den, Riemer Faber, Andreas Beck, and William Den Boer. *Synopsis Purioris Theologiae / Synopsis of Purer Theology*. Latin Text and English translation. Leiden: Brill Academic, 2016.

Bethune-Baker, James Franklin. *An Introduction to the Early History of Christian Doctrine to the Time of Chalcedon*. London: Methuen, 1903.

Billings, J. Todd. *Calvin, Participation, and the Gift: The Activity of Believers in Union with Christ*. Oxford: Oxford University Press, 2007.

———. "United to God through Christ: Assessing Calvin on the Question of Deification." *Harvard Theological Review* 98, no. 3 (July 2005): 315–34.

Blocher, Henri. *Original Sin: Illuminating the Riddle.* Downers Gove: IVP Academic, 2003.

Blondel, Maurice. *Action: Essay on a Critique of Life and a Science of Practice.* Notre Dame, IN: University of Notre Dame, 1984.

Brian, Rustin E. *Covering Up Luther: How Barth's Christology Challenged the Deus Absconditus That Haunts Modernity.* Eugene, OR: Cascade Books, 2013.

Brouwer, Reeling, and Herman, Rinse. "Karl Barth's Encounter with the Federal Theology of Johannes Cocceius: Prejudices, Criticisms, Outcomes and Open Questions." *Zeitschrift für Dialektische Theologie.* Supplement Series 4 (2010): 160–208.

Burnett, Richard E., ed. *The Westminster Handbook to Karl Barth.* Louisville, KY: Westminster John Knox, 2013.

Calvin, John. *The Catechism of the Church of Geneva.* Hartford, CT: Sheldon & Goodwin, 1815.

———. *Commentaries.* Grand Rapids: Baker Books, 1974.

———. *Institutes of the Christian Religion (1559).* Edited by John T. McNeill. Translated by Ford Lewis Battles. Library of Christian Classics 20–21. Philadelphia: Westminster, 1960.

———. *Theological Treatises.* Philadelphia: Westminster Press, 1954.

Cameron, Daniel J., and Myk Habets. *Flesh and Blood: A Dogmatic Sketch Concerning the Fallen Nature View of Christ's Human Nature.* Eugene, OR: Wipf and Stock, 2016.

Campos, Heber Carlos de. *Doctrine in Development: Johannes Piscator and Debates over Christ's Active Obedience.* Grand Rapids: Reformation Heritage Books, 2017.

Canlis, Julie. *Calvin's Ladder: A Spiritual Theology of Ascent and Ascension.* Grand Rapids: Eerdmans, 2010.

Carson, D. A., ed. *The Enduring Authority of the Christian Scriptures.* Grand Rapids: Eerdmans, 2016.

Cassidy, James J. "T. F. Torrance's Realistic Soteriological Objectivism and the Elimination of Dualisms: Union with Christ in Current Perspective." *Mid-America Journal of Theology* 19 (2008): 165–94.

Chiarot, Kevin. "The Non-Assumptus and the Virgin Birth in T. F.
    Torrance." *Scottish Bulletin of Evangelical Theology* 29, no. 2 (2011):
    229–44.

——. *The Unassumed Is the Unhealed: The Humanity of Christ in the
    Theology of T. F. Torrance.* Eugene, OR: Pickwick, 2013.

Clark, John, and Marcus Peter Johnson. *The Incarnation of God: The
    Mystery of the Gospel as the Foundation of Evangelical Theology.*
    Wheaton, IL: Crossway, 2015.

Cleveland, Christopher. *Thomism in John Owen.* Burlington, VT:
    Routledge, 2016.

Cortez, Marc. *Christological Anthropology in Historical Perspective: Ancient
    and Contemporary Approaches to Theological Anthropology.* Grand
    Rapids: Zondervan, 2016.

——. *ReSourcing Theological Anthropology: A Constructive Account of
    Humanity in the Light of Christ.* Grand Rapids: Zondervan, 2018.

Crisp, Oliver. "Did Christ Have a Fallen Human Nature?" *International
    Journal of Systematic Theology* 6, no. 3 (July 2004): 270–88.

——. *Divinity and Humanity: The Incarnation Reconsidered.* Cambridge:
    Cambridge University Press, 2007.

——. "On Barth's Denial of Universalism." *Themelios* 29, no. 1 (2003):
    18–29.

——. "On Original Sin." *International Journal of Systematic Theology* 17, no.
    3 (July 2015): 252–66.

Crisp, Oliver D., and Fred Sanders, eds. *Advancing Trinitarian Theology.*
    Explorations in Constructive Dogmatics. Grand Rapids:
    Zondervan, 2014.

Daley, Brian E., ed. *Leontius of Byzantium: Complete Works.* New York:
    Oxford University Press, 2017.

Davidson, Ivor J. "Pondering the Sinlessness of Jesus Christ: Moral
    Christologies and the Witness of Scripture." *International Journal
    of Systematic Theology* 10, no. 4 (October 2008): 372–98.

Davis, Stephen T., Daniel Kendall, and Gerald O'Collins, eds. *The
    Incarnation: An Interdisciplinary Symposium on the Incarnation of
    the Son of God.* Oxford: Oxford University Press, 2004.

Denlinger, Aaron Clay. "Calvin's Understanding of Adam's Relationship to His Posterity: Recent Assertions of the Reformer's 'federalism' Evaluated." *Calvin Theological Journal* 44, no. 2 (November 2009): 226–50.

Dorner, Isaak August, and Patrick Fairbairn. *History of the Development of the Doctrine of the Person of Christ*. New York: T&T Clark, 1862.

Driel, Edwin Chr Van. *Incarnation Anyway: Arguments for Supralapsarian Christology*. Oxford: Oxford University Press, 2008.

Duby, Steven J. "Divine Simplicity: A Dogmatic Account." PhD diss., University of St. Andrews, 2014.

Edmondson, Stephen. *Calvin's Christology*. New York: Cambridge University Press, 2004.

Eglinton, James. *Trinity and Organism: Towards a New Reading of Herman Bavinck's Organic Motif*. New York: T&T Clark, 2014.

Emery, Gilles. " 'Theologia' and 'Dispensatio': The Centrality of the Divine Missions in St Thomas's Trinitarian Theology." *The Thomist* 74, no. 4 (October 2010): 515–61.

———.*The Trinitarian Theology of St Thomas Aquinas*. Oxford: Oxford University Press, 2010.

Feingold, Lawrence. *The Natural Desire to See God According to St. Thomas and His Interpreters*. 2nd ed. Ave Maria, FL: Sapientia Press, 2004.

Fesko, J. V. *Death in Adam, Life in Christ: The Doctrine of Imputation*. Glasgow: Mentor, 2016.

Fisk, Philip J. "Calvin's Metaphysics of Our Union with Christ." *International Journal of Systematic Theology* 11, no. 3 (July 2009): 309–31.

Garcia, Mark A. "Imputation and the Christology of Union with Christ: Calvin, Osiander, and the Contemporary Quest for a Reformed Model." *Westminster Theological Journal* 68, no. 4 (Fall 2006): 219–51.

Gibson, David. *Reading the Decree: Exegesis, Election and Christology in Calvin and Barth*. T&T Clark Studies in Systematic Theology. New York: T&T Clark, 2009.

Gomes, Alan W. "Faustus Socinus and John Calvin on the Merits of Christ." *Reformation & Renaissance Review* 12, no. 2/3 (August 2010): 189–205.

Gonnerman, Joshua Lee. "Substantial Act and Esse Secundarium: A Critique of Lonergan's 'Ontological and Psychological Constitution of Christ.'" ThM Thesis, University of St. Michaels, 2012.

Gordon, James R. "The Holy One in Our Midst: A Dogmatic Defense of the Extra Calvinisticum." PhD diss., Wheaton College, 2015.

Greggs, Tom. "Pessimistic Universalism: Rethinking the Wider Hope with Bonhoeffer and Barth." *Modern Theology* 26, no. 4 (October 2010): 495–510.

Gregory of Nazianzus. Epistle 101 (Epistle 1 to Cleodonius). In *A Select Library of the Nicene and Post-Nicene Fathers of the Christian Church*, 28 vols. in two series, edited by Philip Schaff et al., series 2, 7:439–443. Buffalo, NY: Christian Literature, 1887–1894. Greek: *Patrologia cursus completes, Series Graeca*, 161 vols., edited by J.-P. Migne, 37:175–94. Paris: Migne, 1857–1866.

Gregory of Nyssa. "Ad Ablabius." Translated by William Moore and Henry Austin Wilson. *Nicene and Post-Nicene Fathers*, Series 2. Grand Rapids: Eerdmans, 1994.

Griffiths, Paul J. *Decreation: The Last Things of All Creatures*. Waco, TX: Baylor University Press, 2014.

Grillmeier, Aloys. *Christ in Christian Tradition: From the Apostolic Age to Chalcedon* Louisville, KY: Westminster John Knox Press, 1988.

Grumett, David. *De Lubac: A Guide for the Perplexed*. New York: Bloomsbury, 2007.

Gunton, Colin E. *Becoming and Being: The Doctrine of God in Charles Hartshorne and Karl Barth*. London: SCM Press, 2001.

———. "Two Dogmas Revisited: Edward Irving's Christology." *Scottish Journal of Theology* 41, no. 3 (1988): 359–76.

Habets, Myk. *Theosis in the Theology of Thomas Torrance*. Burlington, VT: Ashgate, 2009.

Hall, David W. *A Theological Guide to Calvin's Institutes: Essays and Analysis*. Phillipsburg, NJ: P&R, 2015.

Hatzidakis, Emmanuel. *Jesus: Fallen? The Human Nature of Christ Examined from an Eastern Orthodox Perspective*. Clearwater, FL: Orthodox Witness, 2013.

Hector, Kevin W. "God's Triunity and Self-Determination: A Conversation with Karl Barth, Bruce McCormack and Paul Molnar." *International Journal of Systematic Theology* 7, no. 3 (July 2005): 246–61.

Hick, John. *The Myth of God Incarnate.* London: SCM Press, 1977.

Holmes, Christopher R. J. "The Person and Work of Christ Revisited: In Conversation with Karl Barth." *Anglican Theological Review* 95, no. 1 (Winter 2013): 37–55.

———. *Revisiting the Doctrine of the Divine Attributes: In Dialogue with Karl Barth, Eberhard Jüngel and Wolf Krötke.* New York: Peter Lang, 2007.

———. "Revisiting the God/World Difference." *Modern Theology* 34, no. 2 (October 2017): 159–76.

Horrell, Scott, Donald Fairbairn, Garrett DeWeese, and Bruce Ware. *Jesus in Trinitarian Perspective: An Intermediate Christology,* edited by Fred Sanders and Klaus Issler. Nashville, TN: B&H Academic, 2007.

Johnson, Adam J. *God's Being in Reconciliation: The Theological Basis of the Unity and Diversity of the Atonement in the Theology of Karl Barth.* London: T&T Clark, 2012.

———, ed. *T&T Clark Companion to Atonement.* New York: Bloomsbury T&T Clark, 2017.

Johnson, Harry. *The Humanity of the Saviour: A Biblical and Historical Study of the Human Nature of Christ in Relation to Original Sin, with Special Reference to Its Soteriological Significance.* London: Epworth, 1962.

Johnson, Keith E. *Rethinking the Trinity and Religious Pluralism: An Augustinian Assessment.* Downers Grove, IL: IVP Academic, 2011.

Johnson, Keith L., and David Lauber, eds. *T&T Clark Companion to the Doctrine of Sin.* New York: T&T Clark, 2016.

Jones, Paul D. *The Humanity of Christ: Christology in Karl Barth's Church Dogmatics.* T&T Clark Theology. London: T&T Clark, 2008.

———. "Karl Barth on Gethsemane." *International Journal of Systematic Theology* 9, no. 2 (April 2007): 148–71.

Jorgenson, Allen. "Karl Barth's Christological Treatment of Sin." *Scottish Journal of Theology* 54, no. 4 (2001): 439–62.

Kapic, Kelly M. "The Son's Assumption of a Human Nature: A Call for Clarity." *International Journal of Systematic Theology* 3, no. 2 (July 2001): 154–66.

Kapic, Kelly M., and Bruce L. McCormack, eds. *Mapping Modern Theology: A Thematic and Historical Introduction*. Grand Rapids: Baker Academic, 2012.

Kettler, Christian D. "The Vicarious Humanity of Christ and the Reality of Salvation." PhD diss., Fuller Theological Seminary, 1986.

King, Rolfe. "Assumption, Union and Sanctification: Some Clarifying Distinctions." *International Journal of Systematic Theology* 19, no. 1 (November 2016): 53–72.

Krötke, Wolf. "Die Christologie Karl Barths als Beispiel für den Vollzug seiner Exegese." In *Karl Barths Schriftauslegung*, edited by Michael Trowitzsch, 1–21. Tübingen: Mohr Siebeck, 1996.

Kuiken, E. Jerome Van. *Christ's Humanity in Current and Ancient Controversy: Fallen or Not?* New York: Bloomsbury T&T Clark, 2017.

LaCugna, Catherine Mowry. *God for Us: The Trinity and Christian Life*. New York: Harper San Francisco, 1993.

———. "Re-Conceiving the Trinity as the Mystery of Salvation." *Scottish Journal of Theology* 38. no. 1 (1985): 1–23.

Legge, Dominic. *The Trinitarian Christology of St Thomas Aquinas*. Oxford: Oxford University Press, 2016.

Levering, Matthew. *Engaging the Doctrine of the Holy Spirit: Love and Gift in the Trinity and the Church*. Grand Rapids: Baker Press, 2016.

Macleod, Donald. *The Person of Christ*. Leicester, UK: Inter-Varsity Press, 1998.

Madueme, Hans, and Michael Reeves, eds. *Adam, the Fall, and Original Sin: Theological, Biblical, and Scientific Perspectives*. Grand Rapid: Baker Academic, 2014.

Marmodoro, Anna, and Jonathan Hill, eds. *The Metaphysics of the Incarnation*. Oxford: Oxford University Press, 2011.

Mattson, Brian G. *Restored to Our Destiny: Eschatology and the Image of God in Herman Bavinck's Reformed Dogmatics*. Leiden: Brill, 2011.

McCormack, Bruce L. "For Us and Our Salvation: Incarnation and Atonement in the Reformed Tradition." *The Greek Orthodox Theological Review* 43, no. 1/4 (1998): 281–316.

———. "Let's Speak Plainly: A Response to Paul Molnar." *Theology Today* 67, no. 1 (April 2010): 57–65.

McFarland, Ian A. "Fallen or Unfallen? Christ's Human Nature and the Ontology of Human Sinfulness." *International Journal of Systematic Theology* 10, no. 4 (October 2008): 399–415.

McInerny, Ralph, and John O'Callaghan. "Saint Thomas Aquinas." In *The Stanford Encyclopedia of Philosophy*, edited by Edward N. Zalta. Standford, CA: Stanford University, 2016. https://plato.stanford.edu/archives/win2016/entries/aquinas/.

Molnar, Paul D. "Thomas F. Torrance and the Problem of Universalism." *Scottish Journal of Theology* 68, no. 2 (May 2015): 164–86.

Moo, Douglas J. *The Epistle to the Romans*. New International Commentary on the New Testament. Grand Rapids: Eerdmans, 1996.

Muller, Richard A. *Dictionary of Latin and Greek Theological Terms: Drawn Principally from Protestant Scholastic Theology*. Grand Rapids: Baker Book House, 1985.

———. "A Note on 'Christocentrism' and the Imprudent Use of Such Terminology." *Westminster Theological Journal* 68, no. 2 (2006): 253–60.

———. *Post-Reformation Reformed Dogmatics: The Rise and Development of Reformed Orthodoxy, Ca. 1520 to Ca. 1725*. 4 vols. Grand Rapids: Baker Academics, 2003.

Murray, John. *The Imputation of Adam's Sin*. Grand Rapids: Eerdmans, 1959.

Neder, Adam. *Participation in Christ: An Entry into Karl Barth's Church Dogmatics*. Louisville, KY: Westminster John Knox Press, 2009.

Nelson, R. David, Darren Sarisky, and Justin Stratis, eds. *Theological Theology: Essays in Honour of John Webster*. New York: Bloomsbury T&T Clark, 2015.

O'Brien, Peter Thomas. *The Letter to the Hebrews*. Grand Rapids: Eerdmans, 2010.

Owen, John. *The Works of John Owen*. Edinburgh: Banner of Truth, 1965.

Parker, Gregory W. "Reformation or Revolution? Herman Bavinck and Henri de Lubac on Nature and Grace." *Perichoresis* 15, no. 3 (October 2017): 81–95.

Plantinga, Alvin. "On Heresy, Mind, and Truth." *Faith and Philosophy* 16 no. 2 (April 1999): 182–93.

Price, Robert B. *Letters of the Divine Word: The Perfections of God in Karl Barth's Church Dogmatics.* New York: T&T Clark, 2011.

Radcliff, Alexandra Sophie. "The Claim of Humanity in Christ: Salvation and Sanctification in the Theology of T. F. and J. B. Torrance." PhD diss., University of St Andrews, 2014.

———. *The Claim of Humanity in Christ: Salvation and Sanctification in the Theology of T. F. and J. B. Torrance.* Eugene, OR: Wipf & Stock, 2016.

Rankin, William Duncan. "Carnal Union with Christ in the Theology of T. F. Torrance." PhD diss., The University of Edinburgh, 1997.

Riches, Aaron. "Christology and *Duplex Hominis Beatitudo*: Re-Sketching the Supernatural Again." *International Journal of Systematic Theology* 14, no. 1 (January 2012): 44–69.

Romanides, J. "Unofficial Consultation between Theologians of Eastern Orthodox and Oriental Orthodox Churches, August 11–15, 1964: Papers and Minutes." *Greek Orthodox Theological Review* 10, no. 2 (1964): 7–160.

Rowe, Christopher Kavin. "For Future Generations: Worshipping Jesus and the Integration of the Theological Disciplines." *Pro Ecclesia* 17, no. 2 (2008): 186–209.

Sarisky, Darren. "T. F. Torrance on Biblical Interpretation." *International Journal of Systematic Theology* 11, no. 3 (July 2009): 332–46.

Schreiner, Thomas R. *Romans.* Baker Exegetical Commentary on the New Testament. Grand Rapids: Baker Academic, 1998.

Speidell, Todd. *Fully Human in Christ: The Incarnation as the End of Christian Ethics.* Eugene, OR: Wipf and Stock, 2016.

Stam, F. P. van. *The Controversy over the Theology of Saumur, 1635–1650: Disrupting Debates among the Huguenots in Complicated Circumstances.* Amsterdam: APA-Holland University Press, 1988.

Stamps, Robert Lucas "'Thy Will Be Done': A Dogmatic Defense of Dyothelitism in Light of Recent Monothelite Proposals." PhD diss., The Southern Baptist Theological Seminary, 2014.

Strobel, Kyle "Jonathan Edwards's Reformed Doctrine of Theosis." *Harvard Theological Review* 109, no. 3 (July 2016): 371–99.

Sumner, Darren O. "Fallenness and Anhypostasis: A Way Forward in the Debate over Christ's Humanity." *Scottish Journal of Theology* 67, no. 2 (2014): 195–212.

———. *Karl Barth and the Incarnation: Christology and the Humility of God.* T&T Clark Studies in Systematic Theology 27. London: Bloomsbury, 2014.

———. "The Twofold Life of the Word: Karl Barth's Critical Reception of the Extra Calvinisticum." *International Journal of Systematic Theology* 15, no. 1 (January 2013): 42–57.

Sutanto, Nathaniel. "Herman Bavinck on the Image of God and Original Sin." *International Journal of Systematic Theology* 18, no. 2 (April 2016): 174–90.

Svensson, Manfred, and David VanDrunen, eds. *Aquinas among the Protestants.* Hoboken, NJ: Wiley-Blackwell, 2017.

Tanev, Stoyan. "The Concept of Energy in T. F. Torrance and in Orthodox Theology." *Participatio: Journal of the Thomas F. Torrance Theological Fellowship* 4, no. 1 (2013): 190–212.

Tanner, Kathryn. *Christ the Key.* Cambridge: Cambridge University Press, 2010.

———. *Jesus Humanity and the Trinity.* Minneapolis: Fortress Press, 2001.

Thate, Michael J., Kevin J. Vanhoozer, and Constantine R. Campbell. *"In Christ" in Paul: Explorations in Paul's Theology of Union and Participation.* Grand Rapids: Eerdmans, 2018.

Torrance, Thomas F. *The Mediation of Christ.* Exeter, UK: Paternoster, 1983.

———. *Scottish Theology: From John Knox to John McLeod Campbell.* Edinburgh: Bloomsbury T&T Clark, 2000.

———. *Theology in Reconstruction.* Eugene, OR: Wipf & Stock, 1996.

———. "Theosis and Henosis in the Light of Modern Scientific Rejection of Dualism." *Society of Ordained Scientists* 7 (Spring 1992): 8–20.

———. *The Trinitarian Faith: The Evangelical Theology of the Ancient Catholic Church.* Edinburgh: T&T Clark, 1988.

Torrance, Thomas F., and Robert T. Walker. *Atonement: The Person and Work of Christ.* Downers Grove, IL: IVP Academic, 2009.

———. *Incarnation: The Person and Life of Christ.* Downers Grove, IL: IVP Academic, 2008.

Treat, Jeremy R., and Michael Horton. *The Crucified King: Atonement and Kingdom in Biblical and Systematic Theology.* Grand Rapids: Zondervan, 2014.

Trowitzsch, Michael. *Karl Barths Schriftauslegung.* Heidelberg, Germany: Mohr Siebeck, 1996.

Tseng, Shao Kai. *Karl Barth's Infralapsarian Theology: Origins and Development, 1920–1953.* Downers Grove, IL: IVP Academic, 2016.

———. " 'Non Potest Non Peccare': Karl Barth on Original Sin and the Bondage of the Will." *Neue Zeitschrift für Systematicsche Theologie und Religionsphilosophie* 60, no. 2 (2018): 185–207.

Turretin, Francis. *Institutes of Elenctic Theology.* 3 vols. Edited by James T. Dennison Jr. Phillipsburg, NJ: P&R, 1993.

Tylenda, Joseph N. "Calvin's Understanding of the Communication of Properties." *Westminster Theological Journal* 38, no. 1 (September 1975): 54–65.

———. "Controversy on Christ the Mediator: Calvin's Second Reply to Stancaro." *Calvin Theological Journal* 8, no. 2 (November 1973): 131–57.

Vanhoozer, Kevin. "T. F. Torrance's Kataphysical Poetics: How the Incarnation Relates Science to Theology." Carl F. H. Henry Center for Theological Understanding. February 2, 2018. Video of lecture. https://henrycenter.tiu.edu/resource/t-f-torrances-kataphysical-poetics-how-the-incarnation-relates-science-to-theology/.

Vanhoozer, Kevin, and Treier, Daniel. *Theology and the Mirror of Scripture.* Downers Grove, IL: IVP Academic, 2015.

Veenhof, Jan. *Nature and Grace in Herman Bavinck.* Translated by Albert M. Wolters. Sioux Center, IA: Dordt College Press, 2006.

Velde, Dolf te, Rein Ferwerda, Willem J. Van Asselt, William Den Boer, and Riemer A. Faber, eds. *Synopsis Purioris Theologiae / Synopsis of a Purer Theology: Latin Text and English Translation: Disputations 1–23.* Bilingual ed. Leiden: Brill Academic, 2014.

Venema, Cornelis P. "Recent Criticisms of the 'covenant of Works' in the Westminster Confession of Faith." *Mid-America Journal of Theology* 9, no. 2 (1993): 165–98.

Vidu, Adonis. "Trinitarian Inseparable Operations and the Incarnation." *Journal of Analytic Theology* 4, no. 1 (2016): 106–27.

Vos, A. Aquinas. *Calvin, and Contemporary Protestant Thought: A Critique of Protestant Views on the Thought of Thomas Aquinas*. Washington, DC: Christian University Press, 1985.

Wahlde, Urban C. von. and Keith, Chris. *Gnosticism, Docetism, and the Judaisms of the First Century: The Search for the Wider Context of the Johannine Literature and Why It Matters*. New York: Bloomsbury T&T Clark, 2016.

Webster, J. B. *Barth*. Outstanding Christian Thinkers. London: Continuum, 2000.

———. "The Firmest Grasp of the Real: Barth on Original Sin." *Toronto Journal of Theology* 4, no. 1 (1988): 19–29.

———. *God without Measure: Working Papers in Christian Theology: God and the Works of God*. New York: Bloomsbury, T&T Clark, 2015.

———. " 'Love Is Also a Lover of Life': Creatio Ex Nihilo and Creaturely Goodness." *Modern Theology* 29, no. 2 (April 2013): 156–71.

Webster, John, Kathryn Tanner, and Iain R. Torrance, eds. *The Oxford Handbook of Systematic Theology*. New York: Oxford University Press, 2007.

Weinandy, Thomas G. *In the Likeness of Sinful Flesh: An Essay on the Humanity of Christ*. Edinburgh: T&T Clark, 1993.

Wellum, Stephen J. *God the Son Incarnate: The Doctrine of Christ*. Wheaton, IL: Crossway, 2016.

White, Thomas Joseph. *The Incarnate Lord: A Thomistic Study in Christology*. Washington DC: The Catholic University of America Press, 2016.

———. *Wisdom in the Face of Modernity: A Study in Thomistic Natural Theology*. Ave Maria, FL: Sapientia Press, 2009.

Willis, David. *Calvin's Catholic Christology.: The Function of the so-Called Extra Calvinisticum in Calvin's Theology*. Studies in Medieval and Reformation Thought 2. Leiden: E. J. Brill, 1966.

Wittman, Tyler R. "The End of the Incarnation: John Owen, Trinitarian Agency and Christology." *International Journal of Systematic Theology* 15, no. 3 (July 2013): 284–300.

Wyk, W. C., Ignatius (Natie) van. " '... Conceived by the Holy Spirit and
    Born of the Virgin Mary': The Exposition of the Heidelberg
    Catechism in the Light of Present-Day Criticism." *Hervormde
    Teologiese Studies* 70, no. 1 (January 2014): 1–9.

Yeago, D. S. "The New Testament and the Nicene Dogma: A Contribution
    to the Recovery of Theological Exegesis." *Sewanee Theological
    Review* 45, no. 4 (2002): 371–84.

Zathureczky, Kornél. "Jesus' Impeccability: Beyond Ontological
    Sinlessness." *Science et Esprit* 60, no. 1 (January 2008): 55–71.

INDEX

—